# Attainable Sustainability

**Building Your Corporate Climate Strategy**

ADRIEL LUBARSKY

©2023 by Adriel Lubarsky

All rights reserved.

This book or any portion thereof may not be reproduced or used in any manner whatsoever without the express written permission of the publisher except for the use of brief quotations in a book review.

Dedicated to my daughter Mila,
who must inherit whatever we leave to her.

# TABLE OF CONTENTS

| | |
|---|---|
| Introduction | 7 |
| **Chapter 1: What Is Driving Corporate Sustainability?** | **15** |
| Investors | 17 |
| Employees | 21 |
| Customers – B2C | 24 |
| Customers – B2B | 27 |
| **Chapter 2: A Corporate Sustainability Framework** | **33** |
| Measure | 35 |
| Reduce | 42 |
| Communicate | 46 |
| **Chapter 3: Measure** | **53** |
| How Carbon Accounting Works | 56 |
| How to Measure Your Company's Carbon Footprint | 62 |
| A Buyer's Guide to Carbon Accounting Services | 69 |
| Support With Business Metrics | 75 |
| **Chapter 4: Reduce** | **83** |
| Suppliers | 86 |
| Customers | 93 |
| Employees | 102 |
| Energy | 111 |
| **Chapter 5: Communicate** | **121** |
| Employees | 131 |
| Customers | 135 |
| Investors | 140 |
| Climate Frameworks | 144 |

## Chapter 6: Carbon Offsets — 153
- How Carbon Offsets Work — 154
- History of the Markets — 160
- Types of Carbon Offsets — 163
- When Are Offsets Done Well? — 165
- A Buyer's Guide to Carbon Offsets — 172
- To Be (Carbon Neutral) or Not to Be (Carbon Neutral) — 178
- Dos and Don'ts in Communicating About Carbon Offsets — 182

## Chapter 7: Building Internal and Leadership Engagement — 185
- CMO — 186
- CHRO/Head of DEI — 188
- CFO — 190
- CEO — 192

## Chapter 8: Power Wielding — 199
- Trade Organizations — 206
- Direct Lobbying — 207

## Conclusion — 213

## Get In Touch — 217

## Acknowledgements — 219

## Bibliography — 221

# INTRODUCTION

When I was eight years old and growing up on Long Island, New York, about an hour's drive from Manhattan, I learned about climate change in school. The teacher explained to me in fairly simple and non-controversial terms that while the earth's climate changed naturally over time (we had just learned about the Ice Age the previous week!), recent years had seen more drastic temperature changes than any time before, and scientists were fairly certain that human activity was the cause. This was in 2002, when we weren't yet 100 percent confident about the causes of climate change. Either that, or we lacked the political will to say we were.

I was distraught. My planet was changing, and I was barely old enough to have seen the world! It wasn't right. I had to catalyze my circle of influence to make a change. When the school bus dropped me off at home that day, I ran straight to my dad's home office. While I would like to think that I politely knocked on the door and waited to be invited in, I'm sure I just barged into the room and interrupted some sort of important meeting. Nevertheless, once I had my dad's attention, I explained what I had learned. Climate change! Human activity! We must act now!

Dubious about the science but perhaps moved by my passion, my dad asked me what I would like him to do about it. I had already formulated a plan in my mind, so the answer was easy.

"We need to change how we live," I told dad. "Less waste, less pollution. I can't brush my teeth anymore, it wastes water. We need to do the laundry just once a year. And you need to use your car less. So next time you need to go to Manhattan for a meeting, take your bicycle."

These were the parameters I believed I needed to set for my family to do our part to save the planet. If climate change was our fault as individuals, then it was only through our actions as individuals that we could make a difference. Our system is made up of billions of individuals making trillions of choices. We needed to start by changing our choices.

That was the thinking of the nascent sustainability movement of the 1990s and 2000s: if we have a lot of plastic waste, it's the fault of the consumer for buying plastic bottles. If we face a water crisis, it's the fault of the consumer for taking a long shower. If plane travel is shown to contribute gigatons of carbon dioxide and other greenhouse gasses to the atmosphere, punching holes in the ozone and increasing the rate of climate change, it's the fault of the consumer for choosing to fly at all.

Corporations – the ones manufacturing plastic bottles, managing utility infrastructure, and selling jet fuel to airlines – didn't mind this narrative at all. Their hands were clean. If they were guilty of anything, it was giving consumers what they wanted! Consumers *want* cheap plastic bottles. They *want* to run their laundry twice per week. They *want* to fly around the world. It wasn't the company's fault that our actions were causing climate change. It was our fault. Corporations could not be blamed.

The changing narrative over the next twenty years from "climate change is the fault and responsibility of individuals" to "climate change is the fault and responsibility of corporations" would bring with it one of the most cataclysmic changes in business history.

You may have heard the much-cited David Foster Wallace joke about a conversation between fish. Two young fish, taking their early morning swim, meet an older fish headed the other way. The older fish smiles, waves, and calls, "The water's warm today, boys! Enjoy your swim!" And he swims off. One young fish turns to the other and asks, "What the hell is water?"

At the turn of the twenty-first century, we were all young fish. We (particularly the "we" living in wealthy, developed, mostly Western nations) didn't know a world besides one that drowned us in plastic and landfill waste and released toxic emissions into the atmosphere. Perhaps a few older fish could remember a cleaner, simpler time. But to most of the world, pollution was just the cost of doing business.

Bit by bit, a change started to appear in the corporate wall of climate indifference. First, a few small, renegade companies started to talk about the crazy notion that they could do well and do good at the same time. This phase saw climate strategy as corporate morality. Patagonia, the outdoor clothing retailer, started to expand across the nation, promoting higher-quality products that reduced waste and encouraged a connection with nature. Ice cream maker Ben & Jerry's three-legged stool of business decision-making, Planet, Purpose, and Profit, made business headlines as it led the company to enormous growth and a cult-like following. Software companies making historic profits and led by messiah-complex founders talked about their "Don't do evil" missions and moved significant amounts of capital towards renewable energy purchases and climate change conferences. Toyota released the Prius.

These early companies raised the flag of sustainability out of some inner sense of purpose and value. The founders and leaders of these businesses didn't talk about the "business case" or "ROI" of sustainability; they just felt like it was the right thing to do.

At the same time, governments and international bodies began to consider a regulatory approach to tackling climate change. The 1997 Kyoto Protocol called for international action on climate change, with 192 countries signing the agreement (though the signature of the world's largest polluter, the United States, was conspicuously absent). The United States Environmental Protection Agency saw its budget increase from $6 billion in 1990 to over $10 billion twenty years later. American blue-chip companies like General Electric, previously thought to be untouchable by the government, were fined billions of dollars for their role in polluting the environment.

Companies from all industries began to recognize that environmental regulation might be coming for them, too. CFOs and Chief Legal Counsels began to see climate strategy as smart corporate governance. Corporate sustainability was a de-risking and cost-saving strategy, not just a heady Hail Mary from New Age hippie business leaders.

Consumer preferences began to change as well. Environmental documentaries like *March of the Penguins* and *An Inconvenient Truth* won Oscars for showing the world the true effects of humanity's mistreatment of the planet. Increasing climate disasters, from fires in California to flooding in Southeast Asia, began to disrupt lives and supply chains. The bees were dying, Miami was headed underwater, and it no longer snowed in New York City on Christmas. People recognized that some serious changes were happening.

These changes swept the world and began to inspire change and action from company leaders. Executives began to think about climate strategy as a competitive advantage. If a software company could have a climate strategy, perhaps it might be easier to attract young talent. If a beverage company was able to increase the use of recycled plastic in its bottles, perhaps consumers would change their drink of choice. If a sustainability plan developed today could push off expensive regulation tomorrow, then perhaps it was worth the effort.

This thinking brought about the second wave of corporate sustainability. This movement was about companies recognizing the business advantages of sustainability. "Conscious capitalism" and "triple bottom line accounting" became discussion topics at Davos' World Economic Forum, then trickled into boardrooms, savvy investment conversations, and entrepreneur pitch decks. The green transition was happening. Act now, and earn your sustainable advantage! Delay at your own peril! Sustainability was officially a market advantage.

This brings us to the early 2020s. We are nearing the end of this phase as we make our way towards the next step in the transition: climate strategy as regulatory compliance. In the European Union, laws have governed climate reporting for years and large companies have been reporting on sustainability metrics for a decade.

In the United States, we are starting to get there. Already, major investors and global companies require that their portfolio companies and suppliers report on carbon emissions. The federal government requires contractors with over $7.5 million in contracts to report on their carbon emissions. As of August 2023, the Security and Exchange Commission (SEC) is expected to announce within a year a requirement for publicly traded companies to report on carbon emissions. Soon, sustainability will no longer be a nice-to-have or just a smart business advantage; it will be a requirement for every American business. Just as a business can't run without knowing its revenues and expenses, no business will be able to run without a clear understanding of its impact on the climate and a strategy to mitigate it.

To support this transition, companies are appointing different people to lead their sustainability efforts.

Some people make it their whole career. A bachelor's in environmental science leads to a master's in sustainability leads to a Chief Sustainability Officer title with a seven-figure salary. This is a rare but increasingly common way into this world.

Others get involved out of passion. They care for the outdoors and have children who make them think of leaving behind a better world. They work for marketing, engineering, and finance departments but find their way onto volunteer sustainability committees and "green teams."

The third group is required to do it by virtue of their normal work: people on the finance team who are told to get the company ready for IPO, or Chiefs of Staff who are given the assignment because of the CEO's annoyance at being asked the same questions over and over by investors and board members.

Regardless of how you got here, you now recognize that corporate sustainability is more complicated, more scientific, and more nuanced than you may have expected. Unless, of course, you were in the first group who got degrees in this stuff; then you've known that the whole time.

So, how did *I* get here? Since 2014, I've worked in various parts of the sustainability movement, from environmental nonprofits and outdoor-access technology startups to electric vehicles and, most recently, corporate carbon accounting. Since 2021, I've worked with dozens of organizations ranging from small restaurant groups to publicly traded companies, helping them form corporate climate strategies from initial implementation to regulatory compliance.

Sustainability is complicated and rapidly changing, and most companies can't afford expensive consultants or large internal teams. By writing this book, I'm giving you the guide you need to build a successful corporate sustainability strategy; successful in terms of fighting climate change and building a more profitable company. Because without the latter, you'll never be able to fight for the former.

In this book, we're going to unpack what it takes to be a leader in modern corporate sustainability. We'll start by exploring the foundations of the movement, and by focusing more on actual business drivers than on naive beliefs about companies doing good out of a utopian sense of responsibility. This first section is about waking up to the fact that, like it or not, the best way to bring about positive change is to show the world that it's *just good business.*

The rest of the book will be about building a world-class corporate sustainability program. Whether you're a new recruit to the sustainability team at a Fortune 100 company, a college student looking for a compelling argument to defend your climate science career choice to your parents, or an executive at a 500-employee old-economy stalwart, this book's purpose is to give you specific guidance on building your own sustainability program.

As I was writing this book, my wife and I had our first child. As my daughter grows up, she will also learn about climate change. However, instead of hearing about it for the first time from her teacher at eight years old, as her dad did, she will hear about it from her parents, and likely at a much earlier age.

And when she asks me what can be done about climate issues, my answer will have evolved beyond what eight-year-old Adriel believed. Yes, individuals should still choose to bike instead of drive where possible. But when we drive, companies need to make it affordable and desirable to drive electric. Yes, we should waste less and use less water. But when we do laundry, or travel, or buy food, companies need to make it possible for us to make more sustainable choices at acceptable costs.

The actual actions are up to us, but the responsibility of providing options that are both easy and available falls on the company. This book is about helping you set up your company for success in the new green economy. This way, as my daughter grows up, it will be easier for her than it was for her father or grandfather to make the sustainable choice.

*Chapter 1*

# WHAT IS DRIVING CORPORATE SUSTAINABILITY?

Are you ready for sustainability to be a market requirement? If not, you're not alone. Some 78 percent of companies aren't ready for mandatory reporting, according to a 2023 survey reported in *Investor Relations* magazine.

Smaller companies are even less prepared. While almost 71 percent of the S&P 500 reported their greenhouse gas emissions in 2022, fewer than 30 percent of the MidCap 400 did so.

So what's driving this move to mandatory climate reporting, and what are the timelines involved? In this chapter, we'll look at the major forces driving corporate sustainability actions and the different types of requests you might receive. By understanding the motivations of everyone involved, you will be able to build a corporate sustainability strategy that aligns to the demands of different stakeholders.

Let's go back to March 2022, which kicked off a very big year for sustainability in the United States. That month, the United States Security and Exchange Commission (SEC), which is responsible for regulating publicly traded companies, proposed a new climate disclosure rule. It would require companies to report on their Scope 1, 2, and (depending on market capitalization) 3 carbon emissions.

Over the next six months, during the open comment period, the proposed climate disclosure rule received almost 15,000 comments from investors, environmental groups, political advocacy organizations, and companies with opinions on merit and format. This was an astounding amount of interest. For context, an important rule on cybersecurity requirements was proposed just two weeks before the climate rule and, during its six-month open comment period it received a grand total of 144 comments. That's less than 10 percent of its climate counterpart! Clearly there was something important, or at least divisive, about climate regulation.

That summer saw the passage of the Inflation Reduction Act, widely called the most important climate legislation in history. The bill included $369 billion in funding to tackle climate change, distributing the money across sectors like transportation, manufacturing, and environmental justice. Over $200 billion of this money was in the form of corporate tax breaks incentivizing companies to expedite the transition to a low-carbon economy.

Then, in November of 2022, the federal government announced the Federal Supplier Climate Risks and Resilience Rule, which would require major federal contractors to publicly disclose their greenhouse gas emissions and climate-related financial risks and set science-based emissions reduction targets. In doing so, the world's largest buyer (the US Government) put thousands of businesses on notice. These businesses were basically told that they'd better figure out their climate strategies fast, or risk losing their biggest customer.

And finally in April 2023, one year after announcing the proposed climate disclosure rule, the SEC reported a plan to pass the climate disclosure regulation within the year.

All of a sudden, corporate boards around the country who'd viewed sustainability as a nice-to-have corporate social responsibility initiative at best, or dismissed it entirely as a waste of time at worst, started to take it very seriously. 'Figure it out, or lose business' came as an abrupt and considerable threat.

It's important to understand how to respond to these requests, how to prepare your company to comply with new requirements, and how to take advantage of the opportunities that sustainability brings. You'll also want to implement your strategy in a way that actually contributes to the fight against climate change beyond simply meeting regulations and filling out forms. First, however, you need to understand the three forces that have brought us to this point: investors, employees, and customers.

## INVESTORS

In 2022, institutional investor BlackRock made an impressive announcement. Their ESGU ETF, an index focused on supporting companies aligned with environmental, social, and governance targets, was by far their most successful fund. It had 2.6 percent higher returns than other top BlackRock funds. Simply put, ESG (Environmental, Social, Governance) pays.

This was put more gracefully by Larry Fink, BlackRock's CEO of thirty years, in a 2022 letter to CEOs. He wrote, "I believe we are on the edge of a fundamental reshaping of finance. In the near future – and sooner than most anticipate – there will be a significant reallocation of capital… We believe that sustainability should be our new standard for investing."

When Larry Fink speaks, the world listens. BlackRock, with over $8 trillion under management, is one of the world's largest and most successful investors. It has 90,000 registered financial advisors in the world promoting its funds to people, and CEOs everywhere want to make sure they are on Larry Fink's good side. So when Fink shares his vision, CEOs take it as a prophecy and look inward to figure out how they can be a part of the world Fink believes is coming "sooner than most anticipate."

What drove this new change? What did BlackRock know that the rest of the world didn't? Was Larry Fink, CEO of one of the most successful investment firms in history, who built a company into a $100 billion market capitalization, driven by a sudden urge to help the planet? Was he hit on the head and turned into a hippie? Was this man, worth a supposed $1 billion, turning his company into a charity?

Of course not. Larry Fink was simply doing what he had been doing for over thirty years: he was pushing his company to invest in businesses that would be around for the long term. Larry Fink realized early that the world was changing, and that the companies with which he was involved needed to change with it. Oil may have been the black gold of the twentieth century, but it was going to be transitioned out in the twenty-first.

What had happened was that BlackRock started to see a corporate response to a changing climate as more than answering a cry for help from a flower-in-hair generation of do-gooders. The company started to understand that sustainability was becoming a market advantage on its way to being a market requirement. As the company writes on its own sustainability page, "The net zero transition will create risks, but also a historic investment opportunity." One of the world's largest investors realized that there was a market shift happening, and it would be in the company's best interests to pour its money into, and align its brand behind, sustainability.

This market shift in customer preference that BlackRock noticed had been simmering for decades. Eventually, consumer choices drive all investment returns, and it's the job of any good investor to pour money into what they believe consumers want more of. As electronics and improved consumer products were highlighted at World's Fairs and in television commercials of the 1940s and '50s, investors pushed to develop and ship more TVs, refrigerators, and microwaves – oh my! As the world began to shout "globalization" in the 1970s, investors put their money into international factories and supply chains. As consumers demanded cheaper products, investors put their capital behind plastics and low-cost labor markets, which in turn drove up the value of oil, another great investment.

But in the 1960s, books like Rachel Carson's *Silent Spring*, gatherings at Woodstock, and photographs of the environmental destruction of Agent Orange incited a whisper of an environmentalist movement, and in 1970, the Environmental Protection Agency (EPA) was established. Back-to-back energy crises in 1973 and 1979 made clear that our reliance on fossil fuels might not be permanent. The Whole Earth Catalog of the 1980s (read regularly by people like a young Steve Jobs), Al Gore's environmental protests as a senator, and a subculture wave of demands for better food, less consumerism, and more care for our planet began to make clear that people of the twenty-first century had different demands than previous generations.

So BlackRock, the observant investor that it is, decided to push the corporate and investing world to value all the things that people were starting to value on their own. It built up ESG funds, marketed them heavily, and touted its success. In short, BlackRock proved that the customers care about ESG, that people and companies will put money behind ESG, and that ESG pays.

Other investors, following BlackRock's success and seeing the same climate-writing on the wall, started creating their own ESG funds. From 2006 to 2022, ESG ETFs, just one category of ESG investing, grew from $5 billion to $378 billion (see fig. 1.1). If your company wasn't doing the right things around sustainability, you would have a more difficult time raising money than your competitors.

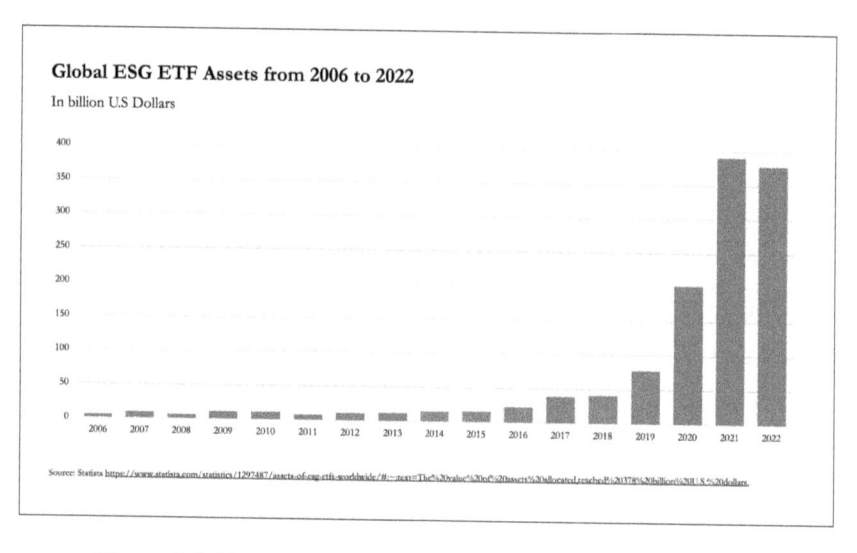

**Figure 1.1.** The growth of global ESG funds from 2006 onwards

As with all good things, the BlackRock story turns out to be as much a story of wisdom as one of warning. Fink taught the world the financial value of the phrase "ESG." BlackRock has built its brand on being the investor of the future; a firm that recognizes and pushes for a more just, clean, sustainable world. The company has created billions of dollars in value by telling people that its funds help move money into the companies that practice modern, conscious capitalism.

But a story from *Bloomberg* on New Year's Eve, 2021, began to chip away at some of those claims. Interviews with Tariq Fancy, BlackRock's former Chief Investment Officer for Sustainable Investing, revealed that the ESG funds under BlackRock were as much marketing as they were truth. "There's no reason to believe it achieves anything beyond sort of giving them more fees, and my concern… is it would be creating a placebo on top of that," said Fancy.

The list of grievances is long, but best highlighted by one statistic. The ESGU fund, BlackRock's flagship ESG fund, holds a higher weighting in twelve fossil fuel stocks than the S&P 500. In other words, the ESGU fund isn't a story of sustainability purity. It's a story of greenwashing, or making sustainability claims your company did not yet earn.

So, what can we take away from BlackRock's story? Is sustainable investment the future or a fraud? Will the trend of increasing ESG fund sizes continue, forcing CEOs to shift business models towards a low-carbon economy, or is this a phase CEOs can ignore?

To paraphrase Martin Luther King Jr., the arc of capitalism is long and bends towards sustainability. If climate change causes the calamities that scientists predict, factories will flood, trade routes will be blocked, and food shortages will cause catastrophic loss. In other words, climate change is bad for business. Investors who buy for the long term recognize that it's their fiduciary responsibility to mitigate climate disasters as much as possible. It's simply good business to lower emissions.

At the same time, we learn a tale of caution. Sustainability requires more than shouting that you care about sustainability. It means more than using the color green in your labels and advertising or building your company's version of an ESGU fund. If you don't hold yourself to high standards, journalists and the public will call you out on it.

## EMPLOYEES

Young people care about the planet. Period, hard stop, end of story.

And while not all young people can work directly to combat climate change (there are only so many jobs, and other industries are equally interesting and important) they want to know that their work contributes to a more sustainable world. They want to know that no matter the industry they are in, and regardless of the scope of work of their day-to-day role, their employers are doing their best to fight climate change.

In 2021, *Forbes* published an article titled "Employees Demand That We Become More Sustainable," which cited a study claiming that 65 percent of workers would be more likely to work for a company with a strong environmental policy.

That same year, a Deloitte study of how COVID reshaped Gen Z and Millennial priorities showed that climate has increased in importance for both groups. It was considered one of the most important issues to address (fig. 1.2).

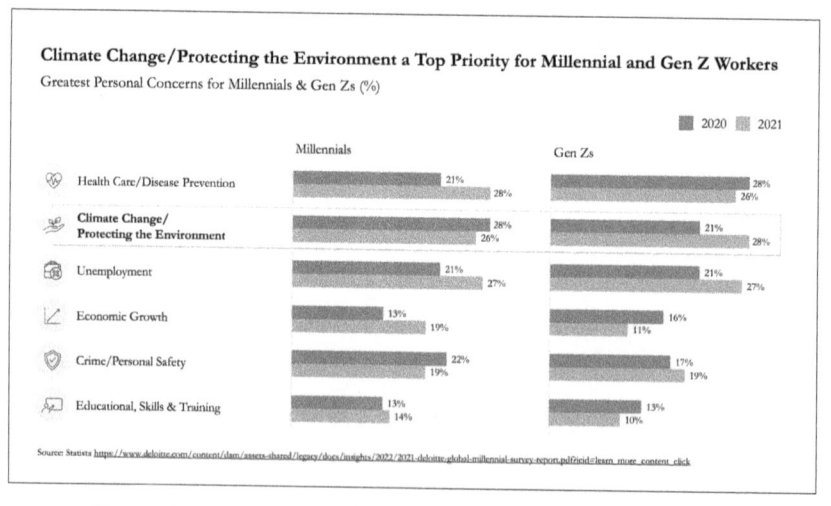

**Climate Change/Protecting the Environment a Top Priority for Millennial and Gen Z Workers**
Greatest Personal Concerns for Millennials & Gen Zs (%)

| | Millennials (2020 / 2021) | Gen Zs (2020 / 2021) |
|---|---|---|
| Health Care/Disease Prevention | 21% / 28% | 28% / 26% |
| Climate Change/Protecting the Environment | 28% / 26% | 21% / 28% |
| Unemployment | 21% / 27% | 21% / 27% |
| Economic Growth | 13% / 19% | 16% / 11% |
| Crime/Personal Safety | 22% / 19% | 17% / 19% |
| Educational, Skills & Training | 13% / 14% | 13% / 10% |

Source: Statista https://www.deloitte.com/content/dam/assets-shared/legacy/docs/insights/2022/2021-deloitte-global-millennial-survey-report.pdf?icid=learn_more_content_click

**Figure 1.2.** Post-pandemic concerns for Millennials and Gen Z according to Deloitte

Deloitte took its own medicine and launched a digital climate course in 2021. Since then, its employees around the world have spent up to forty-five minutes per day getting educated about the latest climate science and what their employer has been doing about it.

Great companies leave employees confident in the knowledge that even if their day-to-day work doesn't address climate change, their employer is acting on their concerns. The *best* companies make caring for the climate part of everyone's job.

This was recently proven to me in an anecdote concerning the social media company Reddit. In November of 2021, I got a call from a Reddit employee who was thinking about starting Reddit's sustainability program. We talked about carbon accounting, ways Reddit could reduce its emissions, and the opportunities for the 'front page of the internet' to play an important role in educating the world about climate change.

A few weeks later, a friend introduced me to John, a former engineer at Reddit. John had worked at Reddit for four years and loved the product, the people, and the work. He was well paid and enjoyed himself. However, as he learned more about the climate crisis, he began to feel like he wanted to play a role in helping people overcome one of the greatest challenges of our time. He looked around at the available employee resource groups at Reddit, spoke with colleagues, and searched through a ton of internal communication. Unfortunately, he couldn't see any way to make the kind of impact he hoped for on climate while working at Reddit. So, in April of 2021, he decided to leave the company without another job lined up.

John spent the next few months experimenting with his own business ideas, learning about climate change and the existing efforts to combat it, and thinking about how to shift his career into the fight against climate change. When John told me his story, I replied that I had recently talked to one of his former colleagues about building out a sustainability program at Reddit. John was happy for the company but disappointed that it had come this late. "If Reddit had this kind of sustainability program a few months ago, perhaps I'd still work there," he said.

A thirty-year-old engineer searching for a role fighting climate change and taking a career risk in the process: This sums up the cost to companies for not taking a stance on sustainability or giving employees a way to contribute.

Companies that create avenues for employees to do their core work while also making a positive impact on climate change will not only increase retention and recruitment, but also get better engagement from employees who are more inspired to work for them.

## CUSTOMERS – B2C

Consumers care about the social causes of the businesses they support and the products they buy.

You probably don't need any facts, charts, or sources to believe that statement. You see it in your own life. You see how the world's biggest brands spend tens of millions advertising what their product stands for as much as what their product actually does. You see it among the Millennial and Gen Z generations who kneel, rise up, and march for causes, searching for movements as loud and powerful as those in which their parents participated.

When consumers shop, they want the very best product for the very best price. But their expectation is that the product they're buying or the business they're supporting is aligned with the social missions and charitable causes that matter to them.

To appreciate the importance of sustainability to consumers and how consumers in America are driving the sustainability movement, you need to understand buying patterns, the so-called green premium, and the impact of social movements.

Consumer buying patterns have dramatically shifted towards sustainability in every category. In food, American consumers spent over $29 billion on plant-based foods in 2020, compared to $2.8 billion in 2015. In fashion, the secondhand and thrift market grew from an $11 billion market in 2012 to a $43 billion market in 2022.

In automotive, electric vehicle sales increased from 10,000 in 2011 to over 450,000 in 2021.

In every single category where consumers have a choice, they have increasingly chosen the more sustainable option. This is, in part, due to the increased investment (and, in the case of electric vehicles, government subsidies) that have helped reduce the cost of the sustainable option.

But even when the costs of sustainability are higher, consumers often choose the more expensive option. The Chief Marketing Officer of Seventh Generation, a company that makes better-for-the-planet cleaning and household products, bragged to the *New York Times* that the premium for their products is usually "no more than 10 percent." And while regular ground beef can cost about $3.79 per pound, the plant-based burger company Beyond Meat has built a $1.1 billion company selling "Plant-Based Ground Beef" at $12.49 per pound.

The green premium, a concept well explained by Bill Gates in his 2020 book *How To Avoid a Climate Disaster*, is "the additional cost of choosing a clean technology over one that emits more greenhouse gasses." In other words, it's the added cost of doing something better for the planet instead of what you might normally do.

What's remarkable about the green premium, as illustrated by products from Seventh Generation and Beyond Meat, is that customers pay it willingly. It might have started because chemical-free cleaning products or meatless burger patties were new technologies that lacked the scale needed to provide a low-cost product. But it persists because customers are happy to make a statement by choosing those products, and companies can capitalize on the added value customers feel like they receive when purchasing a more sustainable option.

Commerce aside, there is a palpable social movement among young people around the world. Climate change, unlike social dilemmas of poverty or illiteracy, is not something that happens far away, in some other land. It is borderless and can be seen by the wealthy and fortunate as clearly as by the poor and unlucky. When California burns, the tech elite of San Francisco see the effects in the sky. When winter comes late, residents all over New York City tell their children stories of a white Christmas that the kids may never see.

Throughout every aspect of life and culture, climate change and the advocates of sustainability pervade. When Leonardo DiCaprio won his Oscar for *The Revenant* in 2016, he told an audience of thirty-four million people, "Climate change is real, it is happening right now. It is the most urgent threat facing our entire species, and we need to work collectively together and stop procrastinating."

Global sports, too, are pushing climate stories to the forefront. In February 2023, players from eighty of the world's largest soccer clubs, including Arsenal, Chelsea, and Liverpool, all wore green arm bands for a week of play. Their aim was to inspire conversation about climate change.

And perhaps no figure has inspired more children than Greta Thunberg, the Swedish climate activist who has a following on X (the app formerly known as Twitter) of almost six million people. As a 17-year-old, she organized the September 2019 school climate strike with over four million participants around the world.

Your customers, wherever they are and however fortunate and safe their lives have been to date, see the impacts of climate change and the conversation around it everywhere they go. Few of them are going to join rallies, work for a climate tech company, or follow Greta Thunberg on strike. Not many can afford the latest Tesla or the cost of rooftop solar panels.

But all of them are aware of the dangers of climate change. They want to act and are going to choose to support the businesses that make it easy to do the right thing for the planet.

## CUSTOMERS - B2B

If your company sells into the Fortune 500, you have probably been asked for sustainability strategies already. If you sell to any of the 2,000 largest companies in America, it's a good bet that sustainability requests from your customers are coming soon.

That's because, as we'll discuss in Chapter 4, one of the first things a company can do to reduce emissions is to push suppliers to set their own climate goals. If Microsoft recognizes that a large portion of its measured carbon footprint comes from the thousands of companies supplying it with products and services, then Microsoft will tell those suppliers to spend time and money figuring out their sustainability strategies. If successful, reducing emissions from its supply chain will then help Microsoft declare a reduced carbon footprint and a win in its ESG report.

If you think about that example, Microsoft didn't do very much. It didn't make any changes itself; it left all of its suppliers scrambling to make a climate plan. And in the end, Microsoft looks like the hero.

A cynic might call it a pass-the-buck cheat code to corporate sustainability. An optimist might see it as a path towards creating systemic change that pushes every company to get involved in the fight against climate change. But a realist, and a capitalist, can't deny that it's just good business to do what your customers care about, and it's very risky to ignore their requests for too long. If one of your biggest customers asks for a sustainability plan, you're going to come up with one. And in turn, that customer gets some credit for pushing suppliers towards sustainability.

Customer requests for sustainability commitments from suppliers are growing. Zendesk, a software company valued around $10 billion, published a 2021 ESG report that showed the trajectory of customer requests for sustainability metrics. The growth is impressive, going from practically zero requests in 2019 to over 20 per year in 2021 (fig. 1.3).

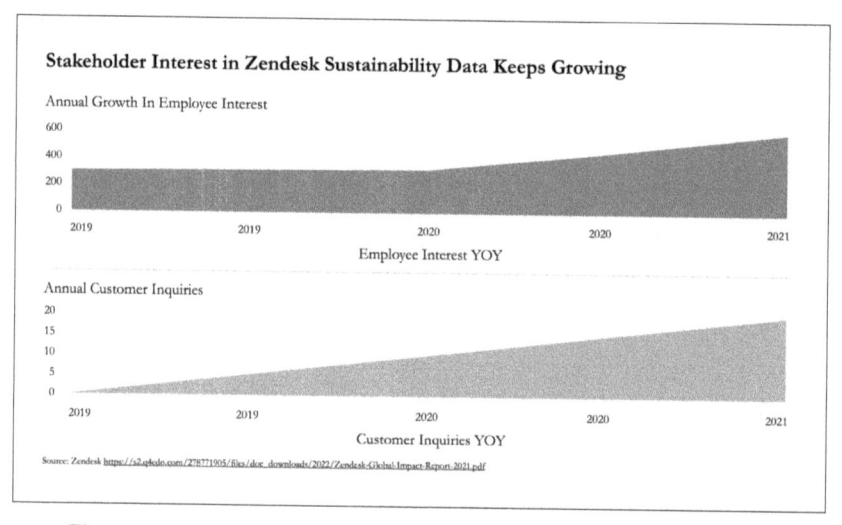

**Figure 1.3.** Growth in sustainability-related inquiries from Zendesk's employees and customers

Because a large portion of a company's carbon footprint is made up of its largest suppliers (the Pareto Principle applies here: 20 percent of suppliers likely make up 80 percent of a corporate footprint), a company looking to engage its supply chain in sustainability is going to make requests of the companies it pays the most. So even if Zendesk, which has tens of thousands of customers, is only receiving twenty sustainability requests per year, those demands are coming from Zendesk's most important customers.

When someone who paid you millions of dollars last year asks you to jump, especially in favor of a popular request like sustainability, you ask how high. And to impress your customer, you might add in a summersault by engaging your own largest suppliers with similar questions, continuing the customer–supplier sustainability pressure.

While Zendesk's 2021 Global Impact Report talked about the demands its customers were making for sustainability, its 2022 report made a commitment to pushing sustainability across its own supply chain. As Zendesk reported,

"Over 90 percent of Zendesk's annual GHG emissions are from our upstream supplier activities. That's why our procurement and sustainability teams are partnering to embed sustainability into our supplier relationships and procurement operations.

- We have added sustainability-related expectations—including disclosing environmental data on an annual basis and setting science-based climate targets—to our Supplier Code of Conduct, which helps our suppliers understand Zendesk's values and expectations.

- In 2022, we started embedding sustainability into quarterly business reviews with a couple of our top strategic suppliers, signaling how suppliers' sustainability progress is valued in our business relationships."

Zendesk started by responding to climate requests from its customers and evolved into asking its own suppliers for sustainability data. The entire ecosystem is moving towards required reporting.

Companies of all sizes are being required to understand and publicize their emissions. This waterfall started with the world's largest companies and is trickling down. Take Robertson Marketing, a 150-employee swag-distribution business that manages the swag programs for big companies like Google and Nickelodeon. While Robertson Marketing doesn't manufacture the swag itself, it helps its clients design products, connects them to manufacturers, and manages the warehousing and logistics.

In 2022, Robertson Marketing got a call from one of its long-time customers, a large global automotive company. They had been working together for over a decade, but now the automotive company needed something it had never previously asked for: sustainability data. This automotive company was working hard to measure and reduce its carbon emissions. Sure, it's crazy to think that emissions from branded T-shirts and water bottles matter much in the scheme of a global auto manufacturer. But the client was being comprehensive, and Robertson Marketing needed to respond to the request. Robertson Marketing needed to measure its carbon footprint to continue giving great service to its customer.

This pushed Robertson Marketing to act quickly. It's not that it hadn't cared about the climate before; the company had existing environmental programs and policies and had done a lot to find more sustainable products. But as a medium-sized, family-run business, it needed to build its sustainability program in parts, growing alongside customer needs.

As owner David Robertson told me:

*"Sustainability is becoming a much bigger deal to everyone. We've been in this business for a very long time, and what has changed is that sustainability years ago felt more like a passing fad, but it's no longer a trend, it's something that's here to stay and it's all-present now. When we work with our best-in-class vendors, the amount of focus that they are putting into the sustainability of their product mix and their own business practices is far beyond what it was thirty or even ten years ago.*

*And they're raising the bar on what they require from their vendors — what they look for in our sustainability program, what information they're seeking from us, and what we report back, including our carbon footprint."*

Many companies are beginning to face similar pressures. Even in corporate cultures where the executive team doesn't want to prioritize sustainability or isn't convinced that taking a stance against climate change is a company's responsibility, things quickly come to a head once customers are on the line.

While consumer pressure is often measured in trends across millions of data points, enterprise customer pressure hits like a sledgehammer. When a customer who pays you $50,000 per year tells you that sustainability is a make-or-break part of your Request for Proposal (RFP), you're going to at least consider how to address it. And when you realize that doing the basics can cost significantly less than the revenue from that single customer alone, the ROI of sustainability becomes obvious.

As we've seen, the corporate sustainability movement is being driven by requests from investors, employees, and customers (both consumers and enterprises). Those investors believe we're in a transition to a green economy and want to back companies that can ride that wave. They're pushing for increased transparency across the global economy.

Employees, too, want to work for companies with a purpose. Sustainability and the fight against climate change are a priority for young people, and they want their companies to contribute to a cleaner, more sustainable world.

And then there are the businesses demanding that their suppliers measure and report on emissions. This is at the core of a corporate sustainability program and pushes the whole economy towards standard reporting.

In the next chapter, we'll look at exactly what a report consists of and the framework that can help you determine what to measure.

## SUMMARY

- The corporate sustainability movement is being driven by requests from investors, employees, and customers.
- Investors are building funds targeting companies seen as sustainable.
- Employees are making decisions about where to work based on a company's commitment to sustainability.
- Consumer preferences are bending towards sustainability.
- Businesses are demanding that their suppliers measure and report on emissions.

## ACTIONS

Conduct an informal survey or a formal materiality assessment of your company's top investors, its employees, and its most important customers. Do investors have sustainability goals on their websites? Are your employees passionate about climate change? Do your customers, as part of a trend or a structured sustainability program, demand progress? If the answer to any of these is yes, you're likely to feel strong pressure to build your own sustainability program soon.

*Chapter 2*

# A CORPORATE SUSTAINABILITY FRAMEWORK

Sustainability, like the Harry Potter boggart, can be described in a million ways. It looks different to each person describing it because it depends so heavily on the context in which it is being discussed.

For example, is a sustainable restaurant one that sources all of its meat within one hundred miles, or one that doesn't sell meat at all?

Is a tech company sustainable by default because many employees work from home and the most destructive part of the business is its data centers? Or is it responsible for the excesses of its well-paid employees, who buy flights, steaks, and cars at rates unseen in other sectors?

Is it possible for a mining company to be sustainable? What if it's mining nickel, a required metal in electric vehicles?

The combination of carbon emissions, and emissions-reduction efforts, are nearly endless. Will your company count as "sustainable" in the eyes of ever-more-discerning markets, or will you be labeled a greenwasher that over-advertises and under-delivers? Or, will your efforts go entirely unnoticed, lost in the noise of today's world?

Over years of working with dozens of companies, I've developed a framework to help any business start and organize a successful sustainability program. In this chapter, I'll introduce my Measure, Reduce, Communicate framework for corporate sustainability. On an annual basis, I propose that companies need to Measure (climate and business metrics), Reduce (internal and external climate impacts), and Communicate (to required and voluntary stakeholders). We'll explore how measuring a common set of climate and business metrics helps companies speak the same sustainability language and builds the case for increased investment. We'll look at how reducing emissions internally and externally helps make an impact on climate. And we'll see how communicating your progress through required reporting and voluntary marketing needs to be done strategically.

Each of these categories has its own nuances. Measurement can be complex and is broader than just a focus on carbon footprint. Reduction can be difficult to implement. Communication can feel like a risk. But without this framework, the job of the sustainability professional is too broad and too undefined to succeed.

Let's take a look at each part of the framework in turn: Measure, Reduce, and Communicate (fig. 2.1).

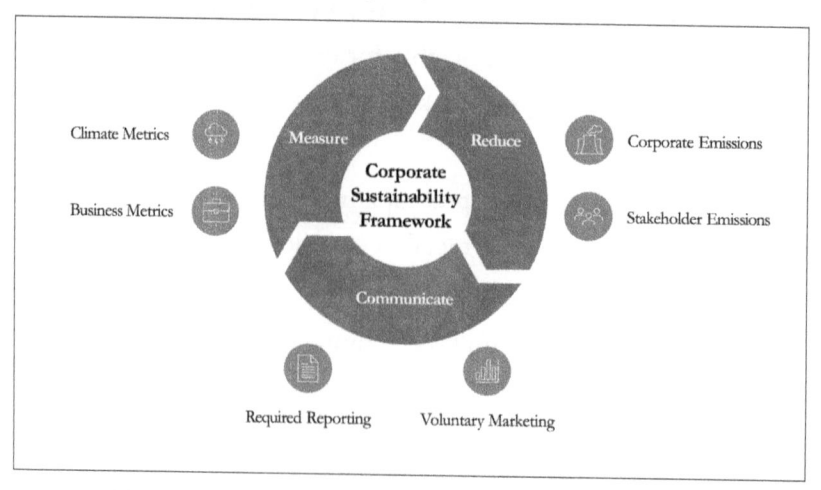

**Figure 2.1.** The MRC Corporate Sustainability Framework

## MEASURE

The first task of any sustainability program is to build a strong culture of measurement. You'll need to measure sustainability metrics to make sure your efforts are impacting the climate. You'll also want to measure how your sustainability program affects business metrics.

Without a clear measurement plan, it can be difficult to assess the success of your sustainability efforts. To what metric do you hold your sustainability team accountable? A reduction in carbon footprint? The number of employees who attend a webinar about climate change? Your stock price? Each of these has as many merits as shortcomings.

Take a company's carbon footprint, for example. A carbon footprint, which we'll be talking a lot about in this book and will explore in depth in Chapter 3, is one measure of a company's impact on the planet. Add up everything a company and its employees do (fly to conferences, commute to work, use energy for offices, buy dinner for clients, pay for cleaning services), then calculate the total carbon dioxide generated by these activities, and out comes a carbon footprint.

A CEO might think that if the sustainability team can lower the company's carbon footprint year over year, they are doing their job and should all be rewarded with lucrative bonuses. Because if the goal of the hippies and scientists you hired to make this whole "sustainability" whine leave your ear *isn't* to reduce emissions, then what are they even doing? But that would be a flawed measure for an obvious reason. If the goal was simply to reduce footprint at all costs, the easiest way to do that would be to fire all of your employees and shut down the company. Voila, the footprint is down to zero and our planet is saved! Obviously that's a bad idea. You do need to have a thriving business, and sustainability should support that goal.

So maybe, then, you should measure sustainability through the lens of ROI. If you're doing sustainability well, then you should be able to market yourself as sustainable, which means customers will pay more for your products. In that case, your sustainability team should be measured purely on the revenue they're helping to bring in. Ask them to report to the Chief Revenue Officer with a quarterly update about what they've done to improve your profit margins. If these tree-loving marketers are worth their salary, they'll do whatever it takes to cement your brand as a sustainable business and convert those efforts into dollars. Right?

But this, too, is misguided. While it is often true that customers and businesses will pay more for products seen as sustainable or coming from purpose-driven businesses, there are obvious examples where a short-term measurement of revenue would put both sustainability and long-term economic growth at risk.

Consider, for example, Best Buy's recycling program. Launched in 2009, Best Buy allowed any customer to drop off nearly any appliance or electronic device to be recycled. As of 2023, this program has helped recycle over 2.7 billion pounds of e-waste. This initiative was unique to its time and remains one of the most expansive corporate recycling programs in the United States. Walmart and Amazon don't offer anything similar, and while competitors like Staples do offer recycling, Best Buy's program is almost ten times larger.

This sustainability effort was not an easy one to set up. The company had to build the marketing machine to inform customers of the initiative, the logistics engine to move products from stores to recycling centers, and the engineering and business development arms to properly recycle and resell components from the millions of devices they would receive each year. If money was the metric, it was unlikely that the people behind this program could have convinced the CEO that it would lead to a short-term increase in revenue or profit.

That would have been extremely shortsighted. Best Buy started with the goal of operating the program at breakeven. Initially, the company required consumers to buy a $10 Best Buy gift card before recycling, to offset the cost of the effort. That requirement was scrapped two years later, as the program became profitable on its own. Over the years, the company used its recycling program to promote additional revenue-generating activities, such as the 2022 announcement that it would pick up any appliance for recycling from your home for $199, and a recycling partnership with Apple that promotes the purchase of Apple products at Best Buy stores.

Best Buy's recycling program is now a pillar of its ESG strategy. If you visit the Best Buy sustainability website, the recycling program is featured as the second bullet, even above the article from Barron's naming Best Buy at #1 on a list of America's one hundred most sustainable companies.

In other words, no traditional business metric would have permitted the launch of this program. But it is obviously a net good thing for the world and for Best Buy's brand and bottom line that the program exists and continues to see innovation and investment.

So, we've discounted measuring either carbon footprint or revenue on their own as a way of gauging sustainability efforts. A good sustainability team will look at a blend of climate and business metrics by which to measure their success. Let's explore the most common examples of each.

## Key sustainability metrics

Getting an accurate picture of your carbon footprint is the most important thing you can do to get everyone in your company aligned behind the same set of numbers. Just as a CFO would never make financial decisions before having a clear picture of a company's balance sheet, no sustainability leader should start coming up with ideas before the company knows its carbon footprint.

Measuring a carbon footprint, a process called "carbon accounting" and explained in depth in Chapter 3, takes time and a lot of quality data. While building a system to collect increasing amounts of primary data for your carbon footprint calculation may seem challenging and time-consuming, it's important to do well. Good data is the pillar of a good sustainability program and will build a culture of measuring and reporting on progress honestly.

Bad data will create two major issues for your sustainability team. First, if your data is inaccurate to begin with, it will be difficult for you to decide which areas you should focus your reduction efforts on. If you only have $10,000 to spend on sustainability, how do you know if you should put it towards making changes in energy or food or employee commuting if you don't know what affects your carbon footprint the most? Without clear data, you cannot begin to prioritize impactful change.

The second problem with bad data is that it takes away a sustainability team's chance to communicate success. There's not a Chief Revenue Officer in the world who would start a meeting with anything except how much more in sales the team has accomplished. The sales department has obvious measurements aligned to it and tangible benefits to the company. That's why CROs and sales leaders are some of the best-compensated people in a business.

So to be successful within a company, sustainability leaders need to think more like CROs. That means finding a way to measure and report on your work with metrics as tangible and analytical as your sales counterparts have, and doing everything you can to tie your team's success to that of the business.

Consider, for example, the case of a sustainability manager I know at a large, private equity owned tech company. Let's call her Sally. For over a year, Sally worked to inspire change within the organization. She met with the CEO to explain that the market was starting to care about sustainability. She put together webinars teaching interested employees what they could do to improve their own personal carbon footprint. She filled out sustainability RFPs when the sales team said they were getting those requests from clients.

But she felt, in her own words, like she was on an island in the company. She wasn't asked to report to the board as frequently as her counterparts. She didn't get as much facetime with the CEO. Her requests for budget were denied more often than not.

Sally's problem wasn't that she was bad at her job. Her problem wasn't that her leadership team didn't care about climate change or that they didn't respect her work. Her problem wasn't that the board, full of executives and investors from other large companies, didn't appreciate the importance of a climate strategy in the market. They all believed that investors, customers, and employees cared deeply about sustainability and that modern successful companies viewed sustainability as a market requirement.

Sally's problem was that no one could measure the benefits of her work. They didn't know when she was doing a good job. They didn't know how to help Sally, because they weren't sure how, or even if, their own efforts could move the needle on her work. And they weren't convinced that her work was as important to the business as theirs. Every company needs sales and marketing and HR and accounting. But do they really *need* sustainability? Or is that just a nice, charitable, feel-good initiative for good times, and a cost center that's easy to cut in bad times? Without metrics, it wasn't clear.

What Sally needed to do was to gather good sustainability data, measure the company's carbon footprint, set her goals to reduce emissions, and regularly report on the company's progress against those goals. If everyone knew what "good" looked like for Sally's team, they'd find ways to help her get there. Everyone knows that more sales is what the Chief Revenue Officer is looking at, so it's easy for product, marketing, and customer success to do whatever they can to get more sales. If everyone knew that Sally wanted to see the company's carbon footprint go down, they'd be able to find ways to work alongside her.

Just like it's important to measure a company's carbon footprint so you can understand the results of your sustainability efforts, a successful sustainability team will also tie their work to building a better business. Let's now look at measuring business metrics through the lens of sustainability.

## Business Metrics

A good sustainability department is one that helps build a great business. There is more to the work than reducing emissions as much as possible. You need to help your company be successful and profitable for a very long time.

The reason that every CEO loves their Chief Revenue Officer in good times, and the reason that the sales department is the last team to be cut in bad times, is because their work is closely and obviously tied to core business metrics. The CRO is positioned directly alongside the company's success. Don't want to approve requested budget for new sales tools? Revenue will suffer, and the CEO will look bad in front of investors. Want to build a bigger, more efficient business? Pay a higher salary for a more qualified CRO. When the CRO wins, the company wins.

Learning from the CRO, the goal of a sustainability leader should be to tie her success as closely as possible to the company's success. Sustainability isn't a nice charity function a company does on the side. Sustainability IS the business. And if the CEO wants the business to grow, they'd better take care of the sustainability department.

Depending on the type of business you are in, you'll want to find the metrics that will inspire your executive team the most. For a public company, you'll want to look at how often terms like "ESG" and "sustainability" and "climate" are coming up in investor calls. Once your CEO becomes aware that they might be asked about sustainability on an earnings call, they'll approve almost any budget to make sure they answer well. A poor answer on an earnings call can be tied directly to a decreased stock price. And if you can prove that sustainability will help the stock price, your CEO will always find the budget for sustainability.

ESG, a phrase first introduced in 2004 by the United Nations to act as a catch-all for a company's Environmental, Social, and Governance initiatives, has skyrocketed in usage. In fact, the phrase was barely mentioned on earnings calls in the 2000s. Then, starting in 2019, ESG conversations grew in importance and urgency. By 2022, one in five earnings calls mentioned ESG (fig. 2.2). From irrelevance to 20 percent of investor conversations in three years is the kind of spike that inspires executives to take things seriously.

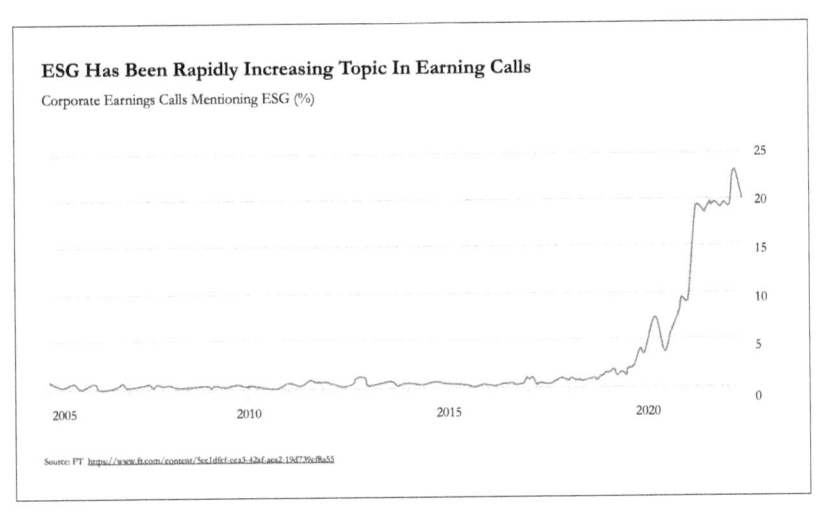

**Figure 2.2.** The rapid increase in mentions of ESG in earnings calls

Business metrics vary based on the company. Consumer brands might measure the effect of sustainability on product price. Supply chain companies might track efficiency and savings. Software companies might measure data storage costs.

We'll explore more examples of business metrics in Chapter 3, because every great corporate climate team needs to understand that they are first and foremost part of a profit-driven business, not a charity team. Keeping an eye on business metrics is going to help build the case for further investment into your sustainability program, and will align your goals with the company's efforts. The financial wind of a strong business case at your back means smooth sailing for your sustainability targets.

Once you've established a culture of measurement, it's time to think about reducing emissions. Let's see how that's done.

## REDUCE

The most exciting (and possibly most important) responsibility of a corporate sustainability program is to reduce emissions. You'll be looking internally at your company's carbon footprint, and externally at the emissions of your stakeholders.

The solution to any complex problem is often simple. Climate change is no different. Want to keep global warming at less than two degrees above pre-industrial levels? Reduce emissions as far as you can go, and remove $CO_2$ for anything you can't reduce.

That's right. The solution to humanity's greatest challenges can be boiled down to four words: reduce emissions, remove carbon.

If the world can reduce emissions at a fast enough rate and remove a significant enough volume of carbon, we can avoid the worst effects of climate change.

Companies and executives enter the sustainability movement for many reasons. Not all of them are as noble and philanthropic as believing in the importance of a company's role in climate change, but it doesn't matter whether you start down this path for reasons of profit or purpose. Motivation matters less than the intensity of action.

The most important action you can take is to help the world reduce its total carbon emissions. If you do this well, it won't matter what your motivation is, as you will be rewarded on every metric. Do this well, and your profits will increase. Your customers will love you. The media will praise you. Your employees will be proud of their work.

And just like that, we can see a genuine path to curtailing climate change.

There are two areas of emissions reduction that you should focus on: internal and external. Specifically, reducing your company's carbon footprint, and helping your stakeholders reduce their own emissions.

## Internal reduction

Most of your reporting will be done against your corporate carbon footprint. That is the metric against which you can take action the fastest and against which you will be judged. Investors will want to know your plans for adjusting to a green economy. Frameworks like the Carbon Disclosure Project (CDP) and the Science Based Targets Initiative (SBTi), which we'll discuss in Chapter 5, will ask about your year-over-year carbon footprint reduction. Customers will ask you for your corporate carbon footprint so they can include it in their own carbon accounting.

With the limited resources of a corporate sustainability team, you'll need to build a plan and prioritize. If you measure your footprint accurately using lots of primary data, you'll be able to understand the biggest areas for improvement. Sometimes, the low-hanging fruit is also the right decision for the business. There are free or low-cost activities your company can take on that will make a genuine impact on your carbon footprint and show quick wins to your leadership team.

Other times, you'll need to do difficult work and take further measurements to set priorities. If emissions from business travel are double the size of the footprint of your employee commutes, but employee commute emissions can be reduced faster, which should you focus on? If it's five times cheaper to switch to LED lightbulbs than to renewable energy, but renewable energy will have ten times the impact, which should you prioritize?

These aren't always easy decisions. Often, there may not even be a correct decision. Most companies just need to do their best to make the biggest difference in the shortest time. Depending on available resources, similar companies may take divergent paths. But for any sustainability program, reducing the company's footprint as much as possible will be its most important, rewarded, and monitored work.

And whatever emissions cannot be reduced must be offset. Understanding the role that carbon offsets play in a sustainability strategy can help your company make the biggest impact it can and recognize genuine benefits from being seen as a climate leader. When used well, carbon offsets help a company reach challenging sustainability goals, build trust among customers and investors, create action in the industry and community, and put a much-needed price on carbon to inspire emissions reductions inside the business.

Carbon offsets are used by the world's largest companies, from Amazon to IBM, and by more local stalwarts, like Hawaiian restaurant group Merriman's and North Carolina coworking space Raleigh Founded. When filtered for quality and used thoughtfully alongside an emissions reduction strategy, offsets can be a legitimate, important part of a climate strategy.

When misused, offsets can also be the smoking gun for calls of greenwashing. Carbon offsets are easy to abuse. If you look at them as your saving grace, to absolve you of all your company's carbon emissions sins, the market will tear you apart.

So you'll need to have a thoughtful approach to carbon offsets as part of your emissions reduction efforts. Carbon offsets are a complicated, nuanced issue and we'll cover them in more detail in Chapter 6.

## External reduction

Great sustainability, however, does not end at your front door. Your business has an opportunity to act as a center for change and influence across your stakeholders. If you can take action to reduce emissions in an area tied to your company, even if it's not reflected in your carbon footprint, you should do it.

Often, this might look like helping your customers with their own sustainability journey. For example, Navan (formerly known as Trip Actions) provides software that helps companies book and organize business travel. It isn't directly accountable for the emissions of its customers' travel, so putting in the work to reduce its customers' carbon footprint from travel wouldn't be reflected in its own carbon accounting. However, realizing that it's still a good thing for our societal goals of combating climate change, the company built a program that helps employees discover less carbon-intensive travel options, from trains that might only add an hour to a trip to lower-emissions flights.

You can also look at how you can support your employees in their personal lives. Many companies choose to make climate education a core part of their employee engagement initiative. By teaching your employees about the climate impacts of eating meat and driving gas cars, and by financially incentivizing and supporting their transition to cleaner and more energy-efficient products like heat pumps and solar panels, your company can build a program that has a genuine impact on the world's carbon reduction goals.

According to the 2023 International Panel on Climate Change report, the world needs to meet some massive emissions-reduction goals in this decade. Climate change is already impacting every corner of the world, and much more severe impacts are in store if we fail to halve greenhouse gas emissions and increase adaptation. Your company has an important role to play, from reducing your own emissions to being a center of change for your stakeholders. The rewards of success – a cleaner planet and a stronger economy – have never been better, and to reap them you'll need to tell others what you've done.

## COMMUNICATE

Your third responsibility in corporate sustainability is to communicate about everything you are working on. Your communication is going to be broken up into two categories: required reporting and voluntary marketing.

### Required reporting

You are going to be required to write certain reports. Your customers and prospects will ask you about your carbon footprint and sustainability targets so they can track their own goals, and your investors will want to know your carbon intensity so they can report to their limited partners. Your biggest customer may ask you to complete the CDP supplier survey.

If you are a publicly traded company, your required reporting may even have a legal mandate. As I write this, in August 2023, the SEC is finalizing its Climate Disclosure Rule which, among other things, will likely require publicly traded companies to report on Scope 1 and 2 emissions.

As a sustainability leader at your company, it will be your job to track all required reporting and make sure your company is hitting its targets.

You will need to maintain tight timelines and push your teams to collect data, even if they don't immediately understand its purpose. Restaurants will need their on-the-ground managers to find the barcodes from every refrigerator in the business. Tech companies will need their HR and communications teams to send out employee commuter surveys. Financial firms will need to organize their investments and portfolio holdings. All of these things may need to happen on tight schedules as your fiscal year end might not give you much time to collect all of the required data.

Take the example of a publicly traded company with a fiscal year ending on January 31. Measuring its carbon footprint can only really begin on February 1, after the books are closed and no additional emissions will affect the carbon accounting. Without any specific deadlines there isn't much of a rush around measuring a footprint, and it can take three to four months if progressing at a leisurely pace. However, this company has a jam-packed spring and summer of required reporting.

It expects to release its ESG report, required as part of its investor relations effort, by May 15. That means the CEO needs the report in hand by April 30, and its accounting firm wants to review all of the data and methodology by April 15.

It takes an outsourced carbon accounting team four to six weeks after all the data is submitted to actually calculate this client's footprint. So the company needs to collect all relevant data by February 28. Consequently, the public company has just four weeks to find data across a dozen offices and over 1,000 employees.

Most companies, even those with well-run sustainability departments, are unable to move that quickly. So how can you get a company up to speed? To find out, I asked Gary Chan at Zuora, the publicly traded monetization suite for modern businesses. Gary is a member of the investor relations team and the person responsible for gathering the data needed for carbon accounting. He told me how he built urgency among colleagues to get the required data quickly and hit such a tight deadline in 2023.

"This was our second year of measuring and reporting on emissions, which helped. We knew where to go looking for data and who we needed to loop in. Teams knew what they needed to get and what we were going to use this data for.

As a value-driven company, our speed came from strong leadership support and engagement in ESG. Our CEO is highly invested in getting ESG right and expected a high-quality report to meet our deadlines. Every time I reached out to teams for data, I'd mention the importance of ESG to our leadership team, in addition to our customers and investors. When we hit a roadblock, I'd escalate to managers to move things along. Leadership buy-in helped inspire teams to get all the data we needed quickly."

But once the ESG report was finished, their work wasn't done. They also had a commitment to report into the Carbon Disclosure Project, a framework that released its extensive survey in mid-April, with a submission deadline of July. So once the ESG report was finished, the investor relations and social impact team went straight into CDP season.

For companies like this, over half the year can be spent on "required reporting." From data collection to impact reports and investor relations to additional climate reporting frameworks, the sheer work of reporting can take the efforts of an entire team.

While reporting is part of the job description of any sustainability team, it's important not to lose sight of the goal. Beautiful ESG reports that are eighty pages long don't actually reduce your emissions. Being part of every single climate organization and framework doesn't actually remove carbon from the atmosphere.

The goal of this mandatory, investor-led reporting is to drive a sense of urgency through the business world and to hold companies accountable to a standard set of metrics.

There are people in the sustainability world who say that all of these reports, and even carbon accounting itself, is a poor use of time. Auden Schendler, who's been the head of sustainability at Aspen Skiing Company for over 30 years, is one of the leaders of the sustainability movement. He would go so far as to proclaim the whole thing to be a sham. Writing reports about what you want to do, and measuring all the flights you are taking, doesn't actually count as doing the hard work to build a better, safer planet. A dollar spent on reporting is a dollar taken away from reduction. Auden is correct.

However, not every company is lucky enough to have a visionary leader who knows what needs to be done for their business and will do it without needing a report to hold them accountable. Most companies don't have someone as passionate about sustainability as Auden. And if they do, then they don't have someone as well-trained. And if they do, then they don't have someone with the same level of seniority. And if they do, their company is still probably not allocating as many resources to the issue as they could be.

In many ways, it is this required reporting that drives the need for good measurement and, in turn, emissions reduction. If investors, customers, and regulators never asked for standardized reports, it is unlikely that so many companies would pick up the sustainability torch as strongly as they have. Many sustainability leaders may see reporting as a waste of time in the urgent crisis of climate change; to them, it might just be moving around numbers and filling out forms. But these forms, when coming from powerful institutions, inspire the need to measure, which in turn inspires emissions reduction. For better or worse, reporting is what is driving 99 percent of action on sustainability.

This sort of required reporting gets us all moving in the same direction. It helps compare apples to apples, create unified policies, and lets companies help and learn from each other. It simplifies things substantially for regulators, boards, sustainability professionals, and researchers. Like it or not, required reporting is here to stay and will be a major incentive for companies to make good sustainability progress.

## Voluntary marketing

The second category of sustainability communication is voluntary marketing. This is all the stuff your company can choose to do to benefit from opportunities in sustainability. Voluntary marketing includes employee engagement, customer marketing, and industry conference talks. These are your opportunities to build your brand among customers, employees, partners, and investors. It is both the largest opportunity and the greatest communications challenge of the sustainability movement.

Your marketing and HR teams are going to love your company's new sustainability efforts. You're going to have less of a challenge convincing them to talk about your work than reining them in so they don't overreach.

Sustainability marketing is booming. Companies who do anything around sustainability tend to do twice as much talking about it, and the appetite for sustainability advertising is massive. Here are just a few anecdotes from a 2021 Digiday report:

For the BBC, between half and two-thirds of advertiser briefs "contain a sustainability element."

Out of Bloomberg's top fifty biggest proposal budgets, about 20 percent are around sustainability. Ad revenue from Bloomberg's climate-focused property *Bloomberg Green* increased 144 percent from January 2020 to January 2021.

The *Financial Times* has seen a tenfold increase in requests for proposals (RFPs) year over year from advertisers seeking to align themselves with the *Financial Times*' climate, sustainability, and ESG content. Of the advertising RFPs the *Financial Times* has received, about 40 to 50 percent mentioned climate or sustainability as a contextual alignment request.

Companies want to talk about their sustainability work, and they are happy to spend the money to do so. This creates many opportunities for the sustainability team to educate stakeholders about new science and practices, bring climate to the forefront of the national conversation, and help the world decarbonize.

Brand-building communication will have you searching for the balance between great marketing – work that inspires and educates your customers or engages your employees in the search for ROI on your sustainability work – and dangerous greenwashing. When done well, this type of communication can grow the value of your stock, reduce deal times, increase customer loyalty, and increase employee retention.

When done poorly, it can result in fines, bad press, and accusations of greenwashing. It will be the job of the sustainability team to review copy in press releases, approve sustainability-related content, and teach your marketers and HR teams how they should talk about sustainability and how to avoid mistakes.

We've seen how tracking sustainability metrics such as your carbon footprint helps your team make better decisions and inspires the company to invest in your work. Tracking business metrics, like investor requests for ESG data, helps build a business case for further investment into sustainability.

Reducing your carbon footprint will involve suppliers, employees, and investment in new technologies. Reducing emissions for your stakeholders, especially customers, is one of the biggest impacts your company can make on climate change.

However, reducing emissions is only half of the battle. Communicating in all required formats is one of the first jobs a sustainability leader takes on. Helping your marketing and HR teams use sustainability as a brand-building tool is a big opportunity, but it has risks if it's mismanaged.

Over the next three chapters, we'll dive into the three parts of the framework in turn: Measure, Reduce, and Communicate. We'll review strategies, examples, and pitfalls in each category to give you the tools to build your own Measure, Reduce, and Communicate plan. In Chapter 3, we'll consider the climate and business metrics a successful sustainability program should be measuring.

## SUMMARY

- Tracking sustainability metrics helps your team make better decisions and inspires the company to invest in sustainability while ESG data further builds the business case.
- Reducing your carbon footprint will involve suppliers, employees, customers, and investments in new technologies.
- Communicating on sustainability helps build your brand for marketing and recruitment and for complying with investor and regulatory requirements.

## ACTIONS

Conduct a review of your company's sustainability program. Are you already measuring climate and business metrics, reducing internal and external carbon emissions, and communicating in required and voluntary channels? Which of these functions is missing from your company? Build your plan to plug that hole.

*Chapter 3*

# MEASURE

As companies recognized their role in the sustainability movement, they began to take action. General Electric, the largest polluter of the Hudson River, invested in clean energy technology. Procter & Gamble, one of the world's largest plastic users, considered alternative packaging. Even software companies with seemingly low emissions put money and engineering into energy-efficient cloud computing. But eventually, these companies stumbled upon the same problem: they didn't know how to measure the impact of their work.

Measurement has some obvious benefits. First among these is the ability to focus. In a large organization, even a low-footprint one like a consulting or software company, there are dozens of factors contributing to the total carbon footprint. Some, like the impact of business travel and the energy used by office buildings, are obvious. If your company wants to make a notable difference in its emissions, there are simple ways to measure the impact of such improvements. Flights can be measured in miles. Convince your team to fly 10 percent less, and you know that you have reduced the company's emissions. And check your energy bill – has it gone up or down? There's a right answer there.

For these companies, the difficulty wasn't just with comparing different kinds of emissions, It was also understanding exactly what they were responsible for. For example, what responsibility does a company have for employees' commutes? Sure, it's obvious that driving to work is probably worse for the planet than taking the bus, but how much worse? And if the company picks up the check at a client dinner or buys the team a branded sweater to celebrate a successful quarter, does that really count as an impact on the climate – one for which the company is responsible?

Proper measurement is the first step in a successful sustainability program. In this chapter, we'll look at how standard climate metrics (obviously) and business metrics (less obviously) can help you build your sustainability strategy. Climate metrics are most often going to look at your company's carbon emissions through the science of carbon accounting while business metrics are going to be useful to drive additional funding and attention to your sustainability program and have an impact on communication.

## Measuring climate metrics

Through the eyes of a corporate sustainability professional, one of the most obvious things to measure is paper use. Back in the 1990s, companies dreamed of a paperless office. They began to invest in computers and require email for all employees. There was confidence in the corporate air that digital experiences would take over from physical ones, and these transitions began to be touted as environmental victories. And, like travel and energy use, it was measurable and infinitely divisible. Did you buy 20,000 fewer cases of paper in 1996 than in 1993? Talk about progress! As sustainability leaders waited for digital technology to usher in a paperless-office utopia, they considered recycling programs an important stopgap. If we must have paper, let it be recycled.

However, even though these categories are measurable against themselves (paper use year over year, flight miles year over year), their sustainability impacts are difficult to compare against one another. Would it be better to get rid of a case of paper or fly 1 less mile? Without a standardized unit of measurement, it's difficult to make impactful decisions.

As the calls for progress on corporate sustainability from investors, customers, and employees became louder, companies needed a way to focus. They understood that some sustainability initiatives were going to be harder than others, and they wanted to make sure that they spent their time and money on the most impactful.

A second benefit to accurate measurement was its impact on communication. While telling employees about a new recycling or clean commute program was exciting (in a nerdy sort of way), any executive knows that it takes more than a memo (paper or digital) to get your employees to change their habits. As investors started to ask questions about ESG and sustainability, it wasn't enough to simply say you were trying to reduce plastic in your product line. Investors wanted to see numbers around that effort, just as they expected data around every other part of your finances.

The need for data fit into how executives were already running every other part of their companies. It would be preposterous to expect a new Chief Financial Officer, tasked with seeking profitability, to do so without a clear understanding of the various cost centers. No one would expect a marketing team to build a campaign without setting specific goals around impressions or return on ad spend. A CEO wouldn't dare go into a board meeting or quarterly investor meeting with broad statements like "We plan on making more money next year" or "We need to hire between 100 and 10,000 new employees." That would be preposterous. So why would the markets allow or expect companies to discuss sustainability progress without an equal amount of data?

All of these factors meant that by the early 1990s, companies were searching for a standard way to understand their own carbon footprints and to strategize the improvements they could make. Around the same time, researchers and climate scientists around the world started making progress in their ability to measure the increase in carbon in the atmosphere.

Standardizing the reporting of carbon emissions began around this time too. The World Resources Institute (WRI) and the World Business Council for Sustainable Development (WBCSD) began to publish papers and organize meetings among leading climate researchers and policymakers to build a standard. Funding came from a partnership with two of the world's largest companies (and largest polluters), British Petroleum and General Motors.

In 2001, the first set of carbon accounting standards was published under the GHG (Greenhouse Gas) Protocol. In its 20 years, the GHG Protocol has had an important impact on how companies approach sustainability. For the first time, the corporate world had a way to think about sustainability in a similar way to how they thought about everything else: through numbers, metrics, and data.

You're probably familiar with the term "carbon accounting," but let's examine it in more detail.

## HOW CARBON ACCOUNTING WORKS

Just like financial accounting, carbon accounting aims to quantify, track, and report on a complex system with enough clarity to help companies make informed decisions. The goal is to have a standardized system so that everyone speaks the same language.

But unlike financial accounting, which has been around since the fifteenth-century merchants of Italy needed a way to track their income and wares, carbon accounting has not had the benefit of hundreds of years of laws, precedents, analysis, and MBA programs to guide it.

At the top of our carbon accounting chapter, it's important to note that the math is imperfect and the system incomplete. Frustration with assumptions, missing data points, and variation in methodology is natural and common. Carbon footprinting is the market's effort to make a one-size-fits-all sustainability metric. Like any such endeavor, it's a flawed system. The carbon footprint of a factory is going to be a lot higher than that of any marketing agency. It will be higher even if the factory is made of fully recycled microplastics taken from the stomachs of rescued sea turtles, while the marketing agency gets every new account executive her own private jet. It's difficult to do an apples-to-apples comparison across very different industries, but the markets have to try. It is the sustainability team's job, and their opportunity, to comply.

So, don't expect perfect science. But carbon accounting is designed with good intent, and resources from the world's largest organizations and most sophisticated accounting firms are being dedicated to continually add to the rule book. And it's the best tool we have today, so let's learn it.

The GHG Protocol divides emissions into three groups, called Scopes, and further subdivides Scope 3 into 15 categories. Scope 1 is fugitive emissions, or the carbon impact of gasses released by industrial appliances like refrigerants, vehicles, and planes. Scope 2 covers purchased electricity, or emissions from powering your offices, factories, and buildings. And Scope 3 covers all the other emissions generated by your business.

As with financial accounting, carbon accounting has many rules. Whoever implements and is responsible for your carbon accounting and reporting needs to have a detailed understanding of the GHG Protocol and all of its guidance around required data, permitted assumptions, and operational control decisions.

Simply identifying the proper category for your emissions can be a challenge. For example, as you can see in table 3.1, if your restaurant purchased a refrigerator during your reporting year, there are multiple options for categorizing its emissions. Your refrigerator will have leakage that needs to be accounted for in Scope 1. It will use electricity, which will be part of Scope 2. And if it is a large, industrial refrigerator, it might also need to be included as a capital good in Scope 3, Category 2.

Whether you decide to use an external supplier for this process or do it yourself (more on this decision later in the chapter), it helps to understand what the different Scopes and categories include so that you can decide for yourself what is most important for your business to report on. This is especially relevant to the 15 categories of Scope 3, as these are all considered "optional" according to the GHG Protocol. Companies may still choose to measure as much of Scope 3 as possible in order to show leadership in sustainability or meet investor or customer requests. Importantly, different categories require different amounts of effort to collect relevant data, so you may decide to roll out Scope 3 over the course of a few reporting cycles.

**Table 3.1.** GHG Protocol Scope Levels 1–3

| Scope and Category | Scope Name | Description | Sample data needed |
|---|---|---|---|
| Scope 1 | Fugitive emissions, stationary combustion, and mobile combustion | Emissions from owned machinery, vehicles, HVACs, refrigerants | Fuel consumption, refrigerant leakage, and other combustion meter data and spend data as available. |
| Scope 2 | Purchased electricity | Emissions from electricity required to run offices, factories, and owned and leased business locations. | Utility bills and square footage of each location. |
| Scope 3, Category 1 | Purchased goods and services | Emissions from anything your business spent money on that isn't included in other categories. Typically the highest-emitting category. | All purchases in the reporting year categorized by spend type (i.e., business service, software, food and beverage.) |
| Scope 3, Category 2 | Capital goods | Emissions from fixed assets (real estate, machinery, vehicles) purchased in the reporting period. | List of all capital goods purchased in the reporting year as well as Scope 1 and 2 data from suppliers. |
| Scope 3, Category 3 | Fuel- and energy-related activities | Relevant to utility and energy companies, this includes emissions from mining coal, refining gasoline, transmitting and distributing natural gas. | Emissions from extracting, producing, and transporting fuel and energy used by your company, most often taken from the Scope 1 and 2 emissions of your fuel and energy suppliers. |
| Scope 3, Category 4 | Upstream transportation and distribution | Emissions from goods shipped by third parties from suppliers to your company's own operations. | Report of all shipped products from supplier to your office that includes weight of items, method of transit, and distance traveled as well as data on fuel used for transport (i.e., amount of fuel used, type of fuel, or money spent on fuel.) |
| Scope 3, Category 5 | Waste generated in operations | Emissions from disposal and treatment of waste generated in operations. | Data on waste produced by operation that might include mass of waste, waste categories, and treatment method for waste. |
| Scope 3, Category 6 | Business travel | Emissions from any travel conducted by your employees. | List of all business travel from employees, including method of transportation (economy flight, first-class flight, train, vehicle), departure location, arrival location, and hotel nights. |
| Scope 3, Category 7 | Employee commuting | Emissions from employees getting to work. Remote work falls under this category. | Commuter survey sent to representative sample of employees asking for average days in office, typical commute method, zip code of home office. |
| Scope 3, Category 8 | Upstream leased assets | Scope 1 and 2 emissions of the operated leased asset that are not already reported in Scope 1 and 2. | List of all leased assets not included in Scope 2, along with relevant utility bills, meter data, and purchase records. |
| Scope 3, Category 9 | Downstream transportation and distribution | Emissions from goods shipped by third parties from your company to your customers. | Report of all shipped products from your company to your customer that includes weight of items, method of transit, and distance traveled as well as data on fuel used for transport (i.e., amount of fuel used, type of fuel, or money spent on fuel.) Optional inclusion of transportation method and distance of your customers traveling to your store. |
| Scope 3, Category 10 | Processing of sold products | Emissions from the third-party processing of products your company manufactures. This is for products you sell to an entity that is not the final consumer. | Waste and energy required to use your intermediate product in the next phase of manufacturing. |
| Scope 3, Category 11 | Use of sold products | Emissions from the third-party use of products your company manufactures. This is for products you sell to the final consumer. | Quantity and type of products sold, expected lifetime of products, expected energy and fuel required for maintenance of products. |
| Scope 3, Category 12 | End-of-life treatment of sold products | Emissions from waste disposal of products sold by your company. | Mass and quantity of sold products and assumptions of the waste disposal method (recycling, landfill, incineration) used at the end of life. |
| Scope 3, Category 13 | Downstream leased assets | Emissions from operation of assets owned by your company and leased to a third party. | Scope 1 and 2 emissions from the entity leasing these assets. |
| Scope 3, Category 14 | Franchises | Emissions from the operation of assets owned by your company's franchisors. | Scope 1 and 2 emissions, from all of your franchisors, or site-specific fuel use, electricity use, and fugitive emissions if you choose not to include this in your own Scope 1 and 2 emissions. |
| Scope 3, Category 15 | Investments | Applicable to investment firms and financial institutions (i.e., banks), this includes emissions associated with your company's investments. | Scope 1 and 2 emissions from any investee as well as a breakdown of percentage of ownership for all investments. |

Carbon accounting lays out guidelines for measuring (and eventually reporting on) your company's carbon footprint. As an absolute number, it's important to know. But it isn't always helpful to know, in a vacuum, how one company's carbon footprint arbitrarily compares to another. Of course, McDonald's has a higher carbon footprint than Marinara's Pizza, a two-location restaurant in my hometown. It's got 20,000 times more restaurants! And obviously Google, with almost 200,000 employees and offices around the world, has a higher carbon footprint than search-engine upstart DuckDuckGo, with fewer than 300 employees.

When absolute emissions are difficult to compare, a more comparable metric, called emissions intensity, is required. Emissions intensity, which measures emissions relative to corporate size, helps investors and sustainability programs benchmark their sustainability programs and is an important metric to track.

## Measuring emissions intensity

If your company is in hyper-growth mode, it's nearly impossible, no matter the industry, to reduce your emissions. If a T-shirt manufacturer is selling and shipping 10 percent more shirts each month, no switch in server providers or investment in clean commuting is going to counteract the growing emissions from shipment and manufacturing.

Even a services business wouldn't be able to reduce overall emissions while growing quickly. If a business hires one hundred new employees in a year, those employees could all be working from homes powered by solar energy and eating vegan porridge three times a day. Yet the company's total emissions are still going to grow as they mail their employees laptops, increase their Amazon Web Services (AWS) storage, and cover the cost of bread, ghee, and organic wine for the holiday party.

In those cases, the job of the sustainability leader is to acknowledge the likely growth in overall emissions and start to track (and try to reduce) the metric of emissions intensity. Emissions intensity can be compared to the Chief Revenue Officer's similar metric of revenue per rep, or sales efficiency. In other words, it divides the company's total carbon footprint across a relevant unit. Carbon emissions per employee, emissions per square foot, emissions per burrito sold.

You can see this metric used in a growing, high-emissions business like McDonald's. If you visit its sustainability page, you'll see that many of its carbon footprint goals are set and measured against emissions intensity.

McDonald's set a 2015 goal to target "a 31 percent reduction in emissions intensity (per metric ton of food and packaging) across our supply chain by 2030." Providing an update on that goal a few years later it said, "As of the end of 2021, the emissions intensity of our supply chain has decreased by 7.8 percent from the 2015 baseline. This means we are approximately 25.2 percent of the way toward our 2030 emissions intensity target at the end of 2021."

While McDonald's absolute carbon footprint continues to increase as it opens new restaurants and sells more cheeseburgers, its emissions intensity decreases. The sustainability team's substantial investments in vegetarian menu options, reduced plastic in packaging, and renewable energy succeed in reducing the emissions intensity of every meal sold and the sustainability team is able to point to major wins. These wins get reported in investor calls (increasing the stock price), consumer marketing (increasing engagement), and employee training (increasing retention). All of a sudden, the sustainability team becomes as integral as the Chief Revenue Officer and can ask for more budget and resources to continue reducing McDonald's emissions. Measuring your footprint correctly, and reporting through the correct lens, is the most important first step towards establishing a sustainability program.

## Additional sustainability metrics

Depending on your industry, your biggest impact on the climate could be metrics that live outside of traditional Scope 1–3 carbon footprinting. Coca-Cola, for example, focuses on water use and sets a goal of reaching 100 percent watershed replenishment. Misfit Markets, the grocery company that merged with Imperfect Produce in 2022, measures what it calls "Scope 4," or avoided emissions, to reflect its contributions to limiting food waste. And Best Buy measures the success of its electronics recycling program, which is not reflected in traditional carbon accounting. While carbon accounting is a good baseline for most companies, many sophisticated sustainability programs will want to think about climate impact beyond their corporate carbon footprint.

## HOW TO MEASURE YOUR COMPANY'S CARBON FOOTPRINT

Companies that want to measure their carbon emissions have two options: they can conduct carbon accounting internally or hire external help from consultants or software companies.

Your company's approach to this build-or-buy decision most often depends on the stage of your business and what you are using this data for. If you are a smaller company or doing this purely as an internal thought exercise, doing your own carbon accounting will save you money and give you a directionally accurate, if imperfect, footprint. If you are a larger business or in a complex industry, using external help will make sure this work is done correctly and will open up access to other sustainability strategies.

But for the first go-round of carbon footprint measurement, called your baseline, you don't necessarily need to have an in-depth GHG report or an accurate measurement of your Scope 3 emissions. In these cases, you're going to be able to get by with a very broad-strokes emissions calculation submitted in a basic spreadsheet.

The advantage of doing your own emissions assessment is obvious. It won't cost you anything besides time. And, depending on how low of a bar you are okay with setting for yourself, it might not even take you much time. If you just Google "carbon accounting calculator," you'll find a few options for basic calculations.

If you are a US-based company with no international operations, start with a calculator from the Environmental Protection Agency (EPA), which you can find by searching for "EPA simplified GHG emissions calculator." The calculator notes that it is built "to help small business and low emitter organizations estimate and inventory their annual greenhouse gas (GHG) emissions." So if you represent a small business, the EPA calculator should be adequate. If you're a larger business you can treat this as a practice round, but don't expect it to stand up well to audits and scrutiny.

Most companies who want to do carbon accounting accurately will hire external help. Because the understanding of the GHG Protocol's standards requires research and education and inaccuracies can lead to accusations of greenwashing, outsourcing emissions calculations ensures they're done right and gives your company a sort of ledger to fall back on to defend any claims. This is especially important for publicly traded companies, as many will want their carbon accounting audited by their usual assurance firm before making any statements to investors.

Even when hiring external support for carbon accounting, it helps to understand how carbon accounting works. This will help you ask the right questions to verify that the partner you're choosing knows what they're doing and will give your team the confidence to dig in, ask questions, confirm accounting practices, and publish results with certainty.

## Primary vs spend-based data

Measuring emissions accurately requires two things: the collection of quality data, and up-to-date emissions factors to apply to them. Data collection is one of the most time-consuming and complicated aspects of this process because of how cross-functional the work has to be. The data required to calculate emissions lives all over your business and it takes a big effort to collect. Collecting data requires identifying what information you need, understanding where in the organization it lives, and convincing the individual or teams in charge of the data to help you access it.

Ideally, you're able to collect primary data for your calculations. Primary data is an accurate representation of what your business actually consumed in a given year. Total miles flown on airlines, total megawatt hours used by offices, total pounds of beef purchased. Accurate data points generate accurate emissions calculations and are the launching-off point for a precise strategy to reduce emissions. They can be hard to get but are important to strive for.

When unavailable, you can turn to spend-based data. Spend-based data considers the amount of money you spend on a good and applies an emissions factor related to that dollar amount. Instead of miles flown on planes, it looks at money spent on air travel. Instead of megawatt hours used by offices, it considers money spent on utilities. Instead of weight of beef, money spent on beef. Spend-based data is better than a random guess but can be very inaccurate.

For example, if two companies each spend $10,000 on business travel flights, the spend-based method would assign equivalent emissions. That may not be accurate if one company took five first-class flights while the other took twenty flights in coach. If one restaurant buys high-quality beef at $12/pound and another buys low-cost meat at $2/pound, primary data will show that every 100 pounds of beef at each restaurant has the same emissions, while spend-based data will make it seem like the quality restaurant has a footprint six times higher than the other.

This example shows the flaws in carbon accounting that you should be aware of early on. To overcome this, try to collect as much primary data as possible and recognize that this isn't a perfect science. A sustainable action, like switching to more expensive, high-quality meat, may not reflect positively on your carbon footprint. Carbon accounting is one important tool in your sustainability toolkit, but it isn't the only and final number.

You'll be able to download a spreadsheet from the EPA's website that will walk you through three steps: defining your operational boundary, collecting required data, and calculating emissions.

### 1. Define your operational boundary

Defining your operational boundary can be a confusing first step because companies have the flexibility to decide what to include or leave out of their carbon footprints.

Scope 3, for example, is optional. Companies who want to publish their numbers in an ESG report may decide that easier-to-calculate Scope 3 emissions, like business travel, are worth including to add more legitimacy and completeness to the report.

A company might also decide that one division, product line, or recent acquisition is outside the scope of its operational boundary. While you have the flexibility to decide what you want to include in your footprint, any of these decisions must be disclosed in your final GHG footprint report.

## 2. Collect required data

Data collection is not going to be easy. Actually, it will suck. The Chief Sustainability Officer of an international restaurant company told me, crestfallen, that when she joined the corporate sustainability world, she believed that she'd be spending most of her time finding ways to reduce the company's emissions, working on new menu items, educating customers and employees about the world of climate change, and doing other spectacularly interesting things. Instead, she spent eight months in data collection, two months in reporting, and, when lucky, two months doing the work she was hired to do.

If you're working with a consultant, they will simplify the process and help you navigate your own organization to collect what you need. Carbon accounting software might make it even simpler with integrations that pull the required data out of your existing systems.

Start by collecting all of the data you're going to need in one place. Don't worry about organizing it yet, that will come later in the process. Here is an incomplete list of data you're going to need to collect:

1. If the company owns planes or private jets, you'll need to know the make and model of the plane and the type of fuel used. Plus, you'll need the amount of fuel used or the total miles traveled or the amount of money spent on fuel.
2. If the company owns any vehicles, you will need to know the make and model of each vehicle. Plus, you'll need the amount of fuel used or the total miles traveled or the amount of money spent on fuel.

3. Office locations (addresses of every office and lists of whether they are owned, leased, or shared spaces).

4. Energy bills for every office. This is easier when you own your office. If you lease and your landlord pays the energy bills, you will need to request a breakout for your specific meters if available. If not, you may request utility bills for the whole building, then apply a proportion of your used square footage compared to the entire covered area.

5. All expenditures from your reporting year. A list of how much money your company spent on anything aside from items covered by other categories. This really means *anything*, from software to cleaning supplies to sweatshirts for employees to food for your restaurant to marketing materials for conferences.

6. Data from all business travel. Ideally, this includes flight numbers, departure airports, destination airports, and seat class (economy, first, etc.) for every flight and similarly detailed data for every train and bus. This should also include vehicles rented by your employees for business travel.

7. Distance that all employees commute to work, frequency of their commute, and method of their commute (car, train, bike, carpool).

8. For any goods shipped to or from your office or stores, you will need the weight of those goods, the distance they traveled, and the mode of transportation.

This data doesn't cover every single category of Scope 3 but should give most companies a good start for a large portion of emissions.

### 3. Calculate emissions

If you're working with a consultant or carbon accounting software, they will take the data you provide and apply emissions factors. International consulting companies and non-profits developed emissions factor databases to include estimated emissions for hundreds of specific activities. They'll list the specific emissions for $1 spent on electronics, or one mile flown on a plane, or one pound of meat.

Emissions factor databases are often expensive, costing tens or hundreds of thousands of dollars. They're meant to standardize this calculation process across the world and do the underlying math of how different countries' energy grids and supply chains may affect the emissions of otherwise similar products. Access to those databases is part of what you pay for when you work with a third party.

If you're calculating your footprint on your own, the EPA emissions calculator has sections into which you can drop all of the numbers you found in data collection. The spreadsheet has formulas built in that will take all of your data (as long as it is converted into the proper metric), multiply it against an emissions factor, and return an emissions output. The EPA has its own emissions factors for many categories, but they aren't as accurate or expansive as what carbon accounting professionals work from.

The output of your carbon accounting work is going to be measured in tons of Carbon Dioxide Equivalents – or $CO_2$e. Everything we do emits a variety of polluting gasses. $CO_2$ is the most common and best known. But others can be much more toxic. Methane is twenty-five times as potent as $CO_2$ and nitrous oxide is almost three hundred times as damaging as $CO_2$. To simplify communication, all of these gasses are grouped together as carbon dioxide equivalents and measured in metric tons (mt).

As you can see, the hardest work is in data collection. There are different ways to calculate emissions without using this specific calculation spreadsheet, as a variety of calculators exist online, and you can try searching for emissions factors to use in your own calculations.

This process takes a lot of work, and there is a risk if you get it wrong. As we'll talk about later, a poorly conducted greenhouse gas inventory can invite accusations of greenwashing. Small businesses who are curious about their footprint, or lack the budget entirely, should definitely start by assessing their Scope 1 and 2 emissions on their own. For larger companies who need a more sophisticated carbon accounting solution, an external partner will be the right answer.

## A BUYER'S GUIDE TO CARBON ACCOUNTING SERVICES

Most small business founders start by doing everything on their own. In part, it's because money is sparse and shouldn't be spent thoughtlessly. Other times, it's because things just don't seem that difficult for a small business owner to do themselves. "Paying for marketing help is crazy. I watch YouTube videos to set up Google Adwords. How hard can carbon accounting really be?"

This is the right approach for a small business. The entrepreneurial owner is correct because unless something contributes meaningfully to the business, or unless there is a risk of catastrophic failure, they shouldn't spend money on it. And for the first few stages, most disciplines really are as simple and straightforward as you think they are.

As discussed above, carbon accounting is similar. Until your company decides to really commit to sustainability, or unless your company is in an industry with complex carbon footprints (manufacturing, transportation), a competent internet researcher can probably use a collection of free calculators, YouTube videos, and EPA blog posts to calculate their own footprint.

After a while, however, that is no longer enough. Once your business reaches the stage of publishing ESG reports and reporting into climate frameworks or is just committed to doing sustainability well, you won't be able to calculate your own footprint. Partially, that is because of how difficult it can be to measure emissions accurately across all three Scopes.

Even if you could measure your corporate footprint on your own, you may not want to. For the same reason that companies retain outside legal counsel or use external accounting and tax preparation services, an external carbon accounting service will create a layer of protection between your company and any ESG commitments it may make and any accounting audits or investor questions.

Lastly, you'll benefit from the scale and support of a well-run carbon accounting service. Most carbon accounting providers work across many clients and provide more climate services than just carbon accounting. You'll be able to leverage their experience to get benchmarking support and know where you stand among your peers, brainstorm and strategize the climate frameworks that make the most sense for your business, get support with emissions reduction strategies, and a lot more.

So, once you've decided that an external carbon accounting service is right for your business, you'll need to explore the many options available to you. While hundreds of companies offer credible carbon accounting, they can be grouped into three categories, simplifying the decision.

In the thirty years that carbon accounting has been around, the world's largest consulting and accounting companies have developed internal practice groups advertising their credibility and ability to handle complex organizations. They have been joined by smaller, more niche climate consulting firms, many of which promote expertise in a specific industry or bespoke ESG service. And in recent years, software companies have started to provide carbon accounting services with a value proposition built on simplicity and data visualization. Let's look at the pros and cons of each of the three options.

## Large consulting firms

Large consulting firms might be the safest choice. Their decades of experience, strong relationships with regulators, and in-house assurance services mean that you are certain to get back a final footprint report that no executive, board member, or regulator will have a problem with. Additionally, in complex industries and for truly global companies, accurate footprinting and quality sustainability strategy require time and resources. Global consumer product companies like Unilever, restaurant and real estate companies like McDonald's, and massive financial institutions like Barclays Bank need the manpower and research skills that only an army of consultants can provide.

On the other hand, you will be paying a high price, as no blue-chip consulting or accounting firm would ever work for less than a few hundred thousand dollars. You will also find yourself spending more time than you might like on spreadsheets, uploading data manually, and retrieving the same information year after year.

## Smaller consulting firms

If you search for "ESG consultant," you'll find hundreds of results ranging from boutique consulting firms with fifty employees to sole proprietors who left their Fortune 1000 sustainability jobs to hang their own shingle.

What these companies lack in manpower, they'll make up for in experience. The people who work here have a focus on, and passion for, sustainability consulting. That means you'll be getting true specialists who can walk your company through the process. Because these are smaller companies, they can often charge a lower fee than their big consulting friends elsewhere.

They'll also have the added benefit of helping you with your emissions reduction and communication strategy. Many of these firms can suggest ways your company can reduce its footprint, assist you in navigating the complex world of carbon offsets, and help you write policies for your business.

The drawback of a smaller firm is a lack of technology and resources. Software, as we'll talk about in the next section, can simplify this process, uncover insights about your footprint, and keep everything organized in a way that spreadsheets cannot. Large consulting firms have the resources to build or buy useful software. Smaller consulting firms lack the capital to develop or acquire it. They need to form partnerships with tech companies to provide their clients with helpful software.

## Software companies

In the mid-2010s, entrepreneurs began to realize that software could make the carbon accounting process a lot easier for businesses. The realization mostly sat on the premise that all of the data needed to understand a carbon footprint could be found inside the business's existing tools. A company's purchased goods and services, for example, can be pulled from any decent expense or accounting software and, with some custom code, be turned into a fairly precise emissions calculation. Instead of searching through executive calendars and expense reports to understand business travel, a company can just integrate its business travel software or upload a data dump into a software platform that pulls all the required data.

As any good software entrepreneur will tell you, an inefficient process that is done in spreadsheets is meant for technological disruption. Chief Revenue Officers have Salesforce. Chief Accounting Officers have QuickBooks. Chief Product Officers have Atlassian. Sustainability leaders deserve their own software.

Entrepreneurs also realized that well-designed software can share better insights and give faster access to data than a spreadsheet-driven consultant. If, for example, a company working with a consultant wanted to understand which of its 20 global offices was most responsible for emissions, it would have to wait a month for the consultant to create some formulas for the spreadsheet, group emissions from energy use, employee commute, and procurement, check the models, and go over the analysis.

With well-designed software, a sustainability manager can click on the office in question and see all of this information immediately.

When they work well, carbon accounting software companies are going to cut your data collection effort significantly and use technology to display data and insights in unique ways. They'll also be significantly cheaper than most consultants, as technology is always more efficient than educated, high-end, white-collar human labor.

What you'll likely lack with software companies, or at least have to pay significantly more for, is help and support. Tech companies are focused on selling software, not consulting hours. So if customers need help with something the software cannot do well, like writing an ESG report, submitting to the Science Based Target Initiative, or building an in-depth decarbonization plan ready to present to the board, software companies may lack the in-house resources to provide this. Or else they will charge extra for them. You need to know what you're buying when you use carbon accounting software. It's software with some services attached, not a full-suite consultant.

So, if you decide that you should be working with an external service to support your carbon accounting and sustainability planning efforts, you can start by asking yourself a few questions:

1. Do we want a consultant or software?
2. How much money do we have to dedicate to sustainability this year?
3. Of that, how much should we dedicate to measuring our footprint?
4. What do I need to accomplish in the next six months to show my executive team / board a clear win?
5. How much support do I need in understanding the basics of sustainability? (If you are an expert, you might want complex software. If you are newer to corporate sustainability, you might want simpler software or a service with more consulting or customer support.)

Once you have the answers to these, decide if a consultant or software is the better option for you. When you set up calls with their salespeople, ask them some of these questions:

1. How many companies like ours have you worked with?
2. How do you support us with the data collection process?
3. How much help can we expect with emissions reduction strategies?
4. How can you help us understand the impact of various decisions on our emissions?
5. What are your security measures to make sure our data is protected?
6. How do you help us benchmark ourselves against others in our industry?

7. What do you know about upcoming regulations that might affect our industry?
8. What do you think are the 1–2 most important things we can do this year?
9. How do you help your clients with employee engagement and marketing?
10. How do you help your clients win executive sponsorship and organize board updates?

You were hired to do the hard work of sustainability, and building a strong culture of measurement in your climate work is an important first step. But, as the saying goes, "no margin, no mission." To keep funding and positive executive attention directed at your corporate sustainability efforts, you'll need to keep track of relevant business metrics. The best thing you can do for sustainability is to tie your success to the company's.

## SUPPORT WITH BUSINESS METRICS

You got into the sustainability business because of a love for the planet. As with all sustainability leaders, you believe companies have a role to play in the fight against climate change, and you want that progress to happen quickly.

But to be successful, you cannot move against the current of financial success. For your sustainability program to be successful, you need your company to be successful. This was proven true in early 2023. Sustainability was on the rise and everyone knew that important regulation was coming. But the economy was in a slump, and companies had to start doing layoffs. A dozen times a day, I would see people with "sustainability," "social impact," and "ESG" roles with the "open to work" banner on their LinkedIn profiles. Even companies fully committed to ESG, like Microsoft, turned to their sustainability departments to find people to let go.

Sustainability programs that can tie their success to that of the business are more likely to receive funding, get facetime with the board, and avoid the "no budget for sustainability in tough economic times" layoff. Successful sustainability programs find proof that sustainability is just good business.

To do so, you'll need to track the business metrics most important to your company. The specific metrics you track depend on the type of company you're working for and their goals at the time, but you'll often find patterns across all businesses.

Your executives care about what investors think because raising money and keeping the stock price high is their primary job. Tracking ESG importance across your current and target investors, like the frequency of sustainability mentions in quarterly calls and the number of investors with sustainability commitments on their websites, will tell you exactly how much money is on the line if your company doesn't get sustainability right.

Even a sustainability leader in a private company should be finding out what investors want to know. Emissions reporting has been growing rapidly among private equity-backed companies, according to a 2021 BCG report (fig. 3.1). Giant firms like Carlyle Group and KKR, and smaller ones like Vista Equity Partners and K1 Ventures, have all started requiring their portfolio companies to report on emissions. If your company is backed by private equity, you can collect data on PE firms of similar size and industries that require companies to report on their footprint. Even if your PE investors don't yet require it, showing this data to your CFO will make clear that there is value in getting ahead of clearly impending sustainability requirements. If anything, having a record of reporting on emissions will make it easier for your current PE owners to resel the business to another firm when that time comes.

**Emissions Reporting Among Private Equity Portfolio Companies Increasing Significantly**

Portfolio Companies Reporting Scope 1 & 2 Emissions (%)

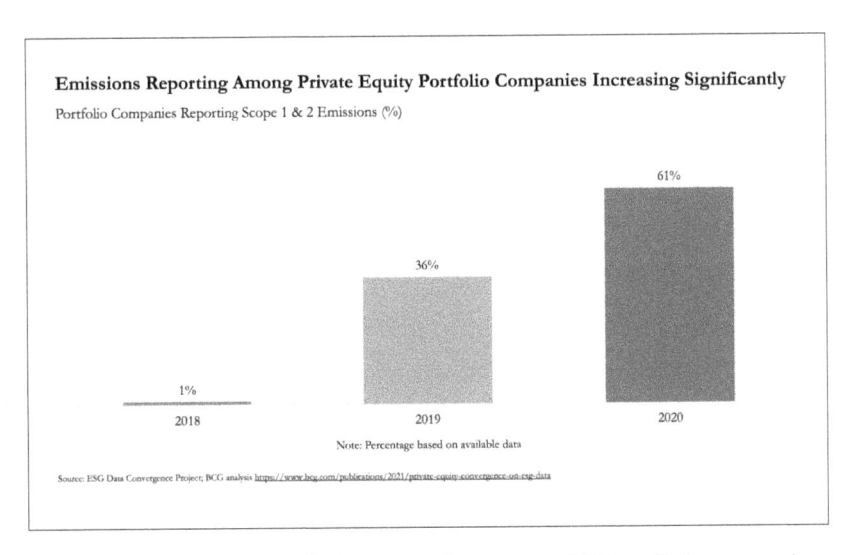

- 2018: 1%
- 2019: 36%
- 2020: 61%

Note: Percentage based on available data

Source: ESG Data Convergence Project; BCG analysis https://www.bcg.com/publications/2021/private-equity-convergence-on-esg-data

**Figure 3.1.** The rise of emissions reporting amongst PE portfolio companies

If you work at a publicly traded company, you may want to keep a list of companies getting fined for improper statements around sustainability. This reverse brag sheet is going to be a hit at board meetings. Make your leaders aware that claims made by underfunded sustainability programs can lead to lawsuits and fines.

In 2021, Allbirds, the running shoe company that built its brand on a low-carbon footprint shoe, had a class action lawsuit filed against it for misleading sustainability claims. The lawsuit argued that the tool it used to defend its sustainability claim didn't consider the entire environmental impact of the shoe. This could have been avoided if the sustainability department had received sufficient investment for its tools and data collection efforts.

Quorn, a UK-based food manufacturer, was disciplined in 2020 by the Advertising Standards Authority for making misleading claims about its own carbon footprint reduction goals. This could have been avoided with a hire on the sustainability team focusing on reviewing all sustainability claims in advertising.

Finding and tracking examples of greenwashing fines relevant to your industry will make sure your CEO, CFO, and board want a sustainability leader in the room reporting on the company's sustainability efforts and claims. Approving budget to be more sustainable feels warm and fuzzy. De-risking lawsuits and avoiding fines is just good business.

In addition to what investors and regulators are expecting, you'll also want to collect data around what your customers and employees think about sustainability. It's easy to find reports and articles about the importance of sustainability to modern consumers, business buyers, and employees. But if you want to build a successful sustainability program that is able to win budget when requested, you should measure the results of your efforts on your company's employees and customers.

If your company has existing Net Promoter Score surveys for either group, make sure sustainability questions are included. Do research on your own, polling employees about how important sustainability is to them and how much they know about your company's sustainability goals. As part of those goals, you're likely to host events and internal educational webinars. Track attendance and engagement at those and use that data to win budget and enthusiasm from your HR department.

You should be similarly methodical about collecting data around customer habits. If you're a B2B business, get some information from your customer success and sales teams about how often emissions data is being requested from your customers' procurement departments. Depending on your industry, you're very likely to see these numbers increasing each quarter, which will help you make a strong case to your leadership team to invest in quality sustainability.

Ask your sales leaders to help you track the number of requests coming in from customers. Create a table that lists your customer's name, the revenue earned from that customer, and the number of sustainability requests they've shared. Every time your sales team adds another row to your spreadsheet, meet with the affected seller or customer success representative to discover the anecdotal details. Did your lack of sustainability data delay the deal? How senior was the individual from your customer who requested the data? How serious did their request seem, on a scale from "just gathering information" to "we've got a mandate to buy from sustainable companies"? Bringing all this data together will help you continue to pitch the importance of a strong corporate sustainability program. It helps you speak the company's language and use good business sense as the driving force of your efforts.

If you're a consumer-focused business, find ways to poll your customers about their preferences, or work with your data science team to track market trends. While it's easy to find data supporting the importance of sustainability to consumers with a Google search, you're going to need primary data that proves this need for your own customer set. If you have an unconvinced leadership team, you need to prove that sustainability matters to *your* customers, not just your *type* of customer.

Start with a set of surveys and polls that ask the customers visiting your stores or exploring your website how much sustainability matters to them. Words matter less than action, so you'll need to take these efforts further. Run tests promoting more sustainable product options for a higher price. Test if your point of sale can be a source for generating donations to environmental causes.

Once you launch the first stages of your sustainability program, continue to collect metrics to prove its value. Quotes and happy customers are good, but you want to find data that is more than just anecdotal. Track to see if customers are willing to pay more for more sustainable products, increasing your company's revenue.

Measure if engaging your customers in upcycling programs can reduce procurement costs. Test to see if word-of-mouth increases around sustainability-focused promotions, reducing marketing costs.

When sustainability is done well, it can increase revenues and cut costs. If your leadership team believes this intuitively, it will seem obvious. But a smart sustainability leader won't rest easy knowing that their current CEO cares about sustainability. That can change on a dime with a new leader or a tough economy. Collect business metrics relentlessly to prove that sustainability is a smart business investment, not just a feel-good initiative.

We've seen how carbon accounting, a system of rules managed by the GHG Protocol, is the first step in building a corporate sustainability program. Paying external partners to do this costs more than doing it yourself but will simplify the process and protect you from mistakes.

You will also want to measure business metrics to make the case for continued funding into your sustainability program. Track customer demand, investor interest, and the potential cost savings opened up by your sustainability program.

Measurement is, of course, just the first step. Using this data to reduce emissions at your company and among your stakeholders is next on your agenda.

## SUMMARY

- Carbon accounting is the first step in building a corporate sustainability strategy.
- External partners cost more but will simplify the process and protect you from mistakes.
- Measure key business metrics to make the case for continued funding into your sustainability program.

## ACTIONS

If you haven't measured your carbon emissions yet, make a plan to do that this year. If you have, increase the number of categories of Scope 3 you are measuring and improve the quality of your primary data.

Identify the business metrics most important to your company, be they increased revenue, reduced costs, improved investor engagement, or something else. Make sure your sustainability efforts move these business metrics in the right direction

*Chapter 4*

# REDUCE

Once you start to see the world through the lens of carbon emissions, you'll see opportunities for improvement everywhere you look. The problem won't be making a difference; it will be gaining the commitment required to make the changes you want to see.

Now that you've measured emissions and tied your sustainability success to the company's goals, it's finally time to build a plan to make a difference in the fight against climate change. This process starts with identifying opportunities for quick wins that show progress to your stakeholders while thinking through longer-term emissions reduction strategies involving your suppliers, customers, employees, and energy use.

Discipline is key to reduction efforts. There's a saying in startups that young companies don't die from starvation, they die from indigestion. Meaning, it's not the lack of opportunity that kills a startup; it's the inability to stay disciplined.

Your sustainability effort is going to face a similar challenge. No matter your industry, there will be hundreds of things you can do to tangibly reduce the emissions associated with your company. So how do you avoid getting caught in paralysis by analysis?

If you are putting together a formal sustainability program for the first time, start by organizing all of the sustainability initiatives your company is doing already. No matter how small the effort, it will help to know everything going on at your company. This will help avoid duplicative work, will let different parts of the business learn from each other, and will be important in creating any ESG reports or updates. External communications are going to want to know the list of things your company is doing in its sustainability journey, and gathering and organizing all of your efforts in one place is the easiest way to start.

Ask your facilities team about existing recycling and composting programs. Ask your legal team about existing policies to encourage low-emissions travel. Ask your procurement and RFP teams what kind of sustainability questions they're asking potential suppliers.

Organizing your work will be a quick, free win that will have a very real benefit for the business. First, it will give your marketing team something to talk about immediately. You'll be able to spin up a sustainability page on your website talking about all of the work your company does to reduce its emissions and position yourself as a leader who has been doing this for a long time because it's just part of your ethos.

It will also be important to the longevity, or what a business school professor might call "business continuity," of your sustainability plan. Often, especially at young companies addressing sustainability for the first time, the job is assigned to one person. That person does their best on a few initiatives for a year or two, then leaves for their next job. All of a sudden, the program is stranded. No one knows what that person did or how they did it. Which Google Drive has the carbon footprint data, which Dropbox contains those pictures of the volunteer event, and which email thread has the details on the new composting initiative? It stalls the program and often forces a restart.

Imagine if every time an accountant left your company, everyone had to scramble to figure out revenue numbers. It would cause chaos and slow growth. That's why accountants use QuickBooks; to keep everything organized and in one place.

Organizing your work in one place is a quick win to show your colleagues the most important opportunities in reducing emissions. You'll see a few things you can easily do more of, and a few simple initiatives that you're not yet doing.

The next step has to be to put some wins on the board. You need to show your peers that you're more than a glorified charity hire for the CEO to wave around on investor relations calls. You are an operator who performs at the highest levels. While it might be exciting to spend the time on a master sustainability plan, a net-zero target that will take fifteen years to achieve, you've got to save that for later. First, your sustainability program needs credibility.

Pick a few efforts that you know will work and that don't need much of a budget. The fewer people involved in implementation, the better. You don't want to be delayed by long approval processes or by others dropping the ball. And you want to make sure that your success is visible to your executives, so they continue to support your work. (There's more on executive support in Chapter 7.)

Steal examples from this book. Many, like improved energy management, sustainable travel policies, and being powered by renewable energy, cost little and immediately reduce emissions. Others, like adding vegetarian menu items, phasing out plastics from the office, and swapping in LEDs for old lightbulbs, require an initial investment but can be tied to long-term cost savings that your executives get excited about. Figure out the initiative that will make a quick impact on your emissions. Get it done fast, then start to work on the next, larger phase of your reduction approach.

While every company will need to find its own path, most can find the biggest opportunities in emissions reduction in four categories: suppliers, customers, employees, and energy. So let's explore each of those, one at a time.

## SUPPLIERS

There are three main reasons that a company turns to its suppliers early in the sustainability journey. Identifying suppliers who are not adapting to a green economy can ensure your company is aware of weaknesses in your supply chain. Getting emissions data directly from your suppliers, instead of making estimates, will increase the accuracy of your carbon accounting (plus, accurate primary data often leads to a lower carbon footprint). And pushing your suppliers to make their own climate commitments creates a systemic shift in the fight to reduce carbon emissions.

One of the main concerns investors have regarding ESG, and one of the main reasons institutional investors are pushing for companies to take sustainability seriously, is a company's climate exposure risk. While investors recognize that a weak sustainability brand is likely to mean a reduced ability to charge high prices and recruit great talent, thereby hurting the company's bottom line, climate risk shows itself most empirically in a company's supply chain.

Climate risk is most obvious in the physical environment. If a retailer sells shirts manufactured in Bangladesh, it is in the retailer's best financial interest to understand how the manufacturer will adjust to Bangladesh's historic floods. If an electronics company relies on a part produced in Turkey, it needs to understand the risk of millions of workers leaving due to climate change-induced droughts and strife.

If a restaurant sources all its bananas from Angola, where only one species of banana is grown, they'd better be aware that if a single drought strikes the country, or if a pest wipes out 10 percent of the banana stock, then that restaurant's best-selling banana smoothies and world-famous banana cocktails are going to be in serious trouble. Investors want to know that companies with physical suppliers are beginning to measure, price in, and address climate risk in their businesses.

This applies to services business by association. While the impact of climate change might not have as strong an effect on a company that builds sales productivity software, its biggest clients are still going to ask for carbon footprint data. In part, this is because all companies want to build a more accurate report of their carbon footprint. Most of their Scope 3, Category 1 emissions (purchased goods and services) are likely estimates. A company may know that its finance department has a line item for $5 million spent on software in one random year, and they might apply a researched emissions factor to that spend-based data, but it is still an estimate.

Without surveying suppliers, there is no way to take into account if your supplier purchases renewable energy credits, reducing its Scope 2 emissions. There is no other way of gathering information on whether or not your suppliers prioritize sustainable practices that curb their emissions. You just can't know if your supplier is helping or hurting your sustainability goals.

The more information a company can get on its suppliers, the more accurately it can understand its own data. And accuracy is important beyond supporting good decision-making. Accurate supplier emissions data can, by itself, reduce a company's carbon footprint.

When your company lacks accurate emissions data on its suppliers (also called primary data) it needs to make assumptions.

Assumptions affect your carbon footprint for two reasons. First, the rules of the GHG Protocol dictate that assumptions are almost always overestimates. Second, assumptions and spend-based data (i.e., how much money you spend on a supplier) don't factor in business realities. If you spend $10,000 on a software supplier, it's unclear if you got a huge discount, bought at a huge markup, or used their emissions-heavy hardware products or their emissions-light software product. An assumption will lead to a high carbon footprint. On the other hand, primary data (asking the supplier for the emissions generated by them serving you) helps you get a realistic value for carbon emissions from using that supplier.

While accuracy is important, true systemic change means no one can be left out of these efforts. Even if your design agency of 200 employees can only do so much to reduce your internal emissions (you're a bunch of vegans who hate travel and work remotely), it sends a signal to the market when a company is able to make a claim that a certain percentage of its suppliers are now committed to measuring, reducing, and offsetting emissions.

So, what can your company do to engage suppliers on sustainability?

The first step is to assess your suppliers. Take a look at the suppliers that make up the majority of your spend (the top 80 percent is a common threshold). Research how many of those have public sustainability commitments, CDP scores, carbon neutrality goals, and net-zero targets. This will help your company learn which suppliers need the most help with sustainability and where to focus your efforts.

Next, set up a sustainable supplier policy. Work with your legal and procurement teams to establish a policy that commits your company to prioritizing suppliers who have made commitments to environmental practices.

Your policy should be tailored to your industry, as a fashion brand that manufactures clothing in Vietnam and ships it around the world will have different suppliers and different opportunities than a vegan restaurant in Brooklyn. But your core components are probably going to be similar. At the very least, you'll want sections requiring compliance with environmental laws and commitment to acting with a certain standard or ethics. To go above and beyond, you may also want to prioritize suppliers with public sustainability commitments. For a sustainable supplier policy template, visit attainablesustainabilitybook.com/suppliers.

The next step is to send your suppliers a sustainability survey. Many companies already have a strict security questionnaire that asks potential suppliers about their data privacy policies, SOC 2 compliance, and history of penetration tests. This is considered best practice to reduce potential exposure to security risks.

Companies who want to push sustainability change among suppliers should begin to ask some basic sustainability questions. These can be added to existing vetting or onboarding surveys and can begin as a very simple set of questions that aren't burdensome for the supplier.

# Sample Sustainable Supplier Survey Questions

1. Do you currently calculate your carbon footprint?
    a. YES
        i. Please enter the time frame of your carbon footprint reporting period
        ii. What are your Scope 1 emissions in Mt $CO_2e$?
        iii. What are your Scope 2 emissions in Mt $CO_2e$?
        iv. What are your Scope 3 emissions in Mt $CO_2e$?
            1. What Categories are covered in your Scope 3 emissions calculations?
            2. If possible, please provide total emissions in Mt $CO_2e$ per Scope 3 Category.
        v. Did you work with a third party to calculate your footprint?
            1. YES
                a. What is the name of the organization(s) that helped you calculate your footprint?
            2. NO
2. Has your company reported into any notable climate frameworks?
    a. YES
        i. Which ones? Select all that apply
            1. Net Zero / SBTi
            2. CDP
            3. TCFD
            4. GRI
            5. Other: _____
    b. NO
3. Does your company have a carbon neutrality goal?
    a. YES, we are currently carbon neutral
    b. YES, we will be carbon neutral by <u>YEAR</u>
    c. NO
4. Has your company set any sustainability targets (i.e., emissions reduction targets)?
    a. YES
        i. Describe them
    b. NO
5. What percentage of your energy is powered by renewables?

Your first few years of implementing these policies and surveys shouldn't come with punishments. You're just trying to make clear to your supplier network that sustainability is important and should be top of mind for them. Help them set some timelines and goals around their climate reporting efforts. Ask if they can measure at least their Scope 1 and 2 footprints in the next 12 months. Be a partner to them and share education and resources to help them do this.

Over time, you can become stricter with your requests, more stringent with your punishments, and more encouraging with your rewards.

In its *Climate Action Plan,* Salesforce set a very real call to action for its suppliers, committing them to set targets by a certain date (fig. 4.1). The plan says:

"We've committed that suppliers representing 60 percent of our Scope 3 greenhouse gas emissions will set their own science-based targets (SBTs) by FY25, and we are invested in supporting our suppliers in achieving their targets."

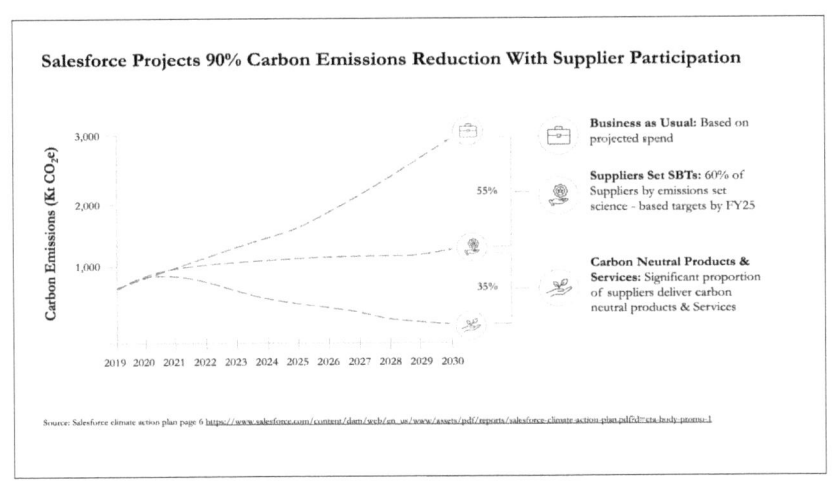

**Figure 4.1** Salesforce's projected carbon emissions

Salesforce is going to help its suppliers accomplish this by providing resources and services. And while not every company can ask as much of its suppliers as a Fortune 500 company, you can incentivize your suppliers to whatever level feels appropriate.

In the pharmaceutical industry, it's becoming increasingly popular to ask suppliers to adhere to CDP. Novo Nordisk, a Danish pharmaceutical company, asked all its suppliers to do this in 2022. Many pushed back, saying that they were unable to meet the request that year. There was just too much those companies hadn't yet done. So Novo Nordisk took this to heart and pushed its request back by a year. That gave its suppliers time to begin measuring their footprints and preparing for CDP submissions in 2023.

At least in its first year, Novo Nordisk won't be punishing suppliers for a low CDP score. It's more interested in getting all its suppliers to take climate change seriously and inspire positive change. But within the next few years, it is likely to begin implementing an incentive program for companies that meet certain targets and a divestment from companies not prioritizing sustainability.

When these supplier surveys and policies work well, they show executives from all industries that sustainability is just good business. Executives who might be hesitant to prioritize sustainability normally, and are waiting for slow regulation to require it, will be moved to faster action by the rapid and economic-driven push of customer demand.

It's even better when you actually help your suppliers reach their goals. If you want more companies to measure their carbon footprint, work out a referral deal with your own carbon accounting provider and recommend them to your suppliers. If you want more companies to be carbon neutral, create an offset buying group so you can purchase carbon offsets in bulk at a discounted rate. If you want more companies to use renewable energy, send them clear guides to navigating the process. Don't expect everyone to have your level of commitment, expertise, or capital to put towards this work.

The goal of these policies is not, however, to force a burden on your suppliers or to make them see the world through your lens. You're not demanding conformity. Net zero commitments aren't a fit for everyone, and carbon neutrality has a very real financial cost that not every company can swallow at the same pace. You can push and prod and incentivize and ask. And you should work with your biggest suppliers, the companies that have the largest impact on your carbon footprint, to set longer-term targets. But don't demand change for tomorrow. It might backfire and anger your suppliers or force them into commitments they're not ready to see through. Show empathy and support and join your suppliers for the journey.

Helping your suppliers reduce their emissions will reflect well on your internal carbon footprint and help move your whole industry towards sustainability. Working with your customers to help them reduce their emissions, whether or not this appears on your internal carbon footprint, will help your company play an important role in the global decarbonization and sustainability-education movement.

## CUSTOMERS

Your company's sustainability strategy is never more visible than in your interactions with customers. It's where your products and services meet the real world, and where your brand is judged and rated for its commitments. If you can help customers make more sustainable choices through your business, or help them reduce emissions in other areas of their lives, your sustainability program will be successful.

There are two categories of customer-related emissions-reduction strategies that are distinct from what we've already discussed in relation to suppliers. The first is to create more sustainable products for your customers that reduce your business's emissions (reducing internal emissions). The second is to help your customer make sustainable choices that may not be reflected in your own carbon emissions (reducing external emissions). In the first approach, you create options for your customers. In the second, you become a platform for change.

## Reduce emissions of your own products

Think back to how you felt whenever you opened a delivery wrapped in plastic and stuffed with Styrofoam packing peanuts. It was waste on display and spoke loudly about the seller who cared so little for the environment. Customers hated to see that waste and devalued those brands in their minds. As a result, companies have responded and invested in improved packaging. Those changes weren't easy. It costs money to test and deploy new boxes and packaging innovations. They had to hire teams, consultants, and engineers.

But after years of effort from the industry, inspired by passionate customers, that Styrofoam-peanut reality of the past twenty years is basically history.

One of the most visible options for sustainable change comes from the restaurant industry. In the twentieth century, menus rarely considered a vegetarian diet. In the 1990s, some restaurants may have started to offer a few bland vegetarian dishes to accommodate the fad that was eating less meat. But as vegetarianism grew as both a health and a sustainability movement, restaurants realized it was good for business and good for their carbon footprints to offer more meatless choices.

Taco Bell did this very well. Serving Mexican cuisine, its menu was able to adopt vegetarian dishes quite naturally. The sustainability team worked to make vegetarian proteins like black beans and sweet potatoes a free substitute for any meat. Their goal was to help customers choose a lower-emissions product (meatless meals) without any sacrifice in quality or taste. The team created "Veggie Mode" on the checkout kiosk to make it easier for customers to choose the vegetarian option and found that they loved how easy it was to try meatless options.

Just Salad, a New York-based fast-casual salad chain, gave its customers an emissions-reducing option outside of low-carbon food choices. Its sustainability team developed a reusable salad bowl. They conducted a life cycle assessment (a sort of carbon footprint on a physical product) on the bowl and found that it had about the same emissions as two normal disposable bowls. So they gave customers the option of buying the reusable Just Salad bowl and receiving a discount on future orders, or staying with the disposable bowls. This option, paired with the discount incentive, was a hit for their most loyal customers and gave customers and the company a way to reduce emissions.

Just Salad used its platform to push for an even bigger option on behalf of customers. For decades, every takeout order would come with enough chopsticks, napkins, and plastic silverware to serve a small militia. It created an immense amount of waste, annoyance for customers, and cost for businesses. But that began to change with environmental pushes from companies.

In 2019, Uber Eats responded to thousands of emails from customers and environmental groups decrying the estimated forty billion pounds of plastic waste that comes from single-use utensils each year. The company created a flow on their checkout page that made plastic silverware and napkins optional, and opt-in. This took effort working with restaurants and redesigning their app but resulted in almost a billion fewer utensils used per year worldwide.

The Just Salad team went even further to make these options a requirement through a strategy called power wielding, which we'll explore in Chapter 8. The team lobbied the city of New York to pass Local Law 17 in 2023, nicknamed the "Skip the Stuff" bill. The bill required restaurants and other food service establishments to only provide napkins and utensils upon request. These changes would make a dent in the 20,000 tons of annual plastic waste produced by NYC residents, help restaurants save an estimated $3,000–$21,000 per year, and put brands like Just Salad at the forefront of sustainability news and conversations.

When Lyft launched its Green Mode in April 2023, making it easy for customers to order an electric vehicle instead of an internal combustion car, it was an attempt to offer customers a lower-emissions alternative and reduce their corporate carbon footprint. When Hilton Hotels asked customers to hang towels they didn't want washed, it was to offer a lower-emissions option that would reduce their corporate carbon footprint. When White Castle offered plant-based burgers, when Amazon launched Amazon Day delivery to consolidate drop-offs, and when Apple launched Clean Energy Charging on the iPhone, each company gave customers the option to pick a more sustainable version of their product that would lower its carbon footprint.

Often, the most obvious sustainability emissions reduction you can make requires innovating your offering so that customers can buy your lowest-emissions products. But sometimes, you need to focus your business on becoming a platform for wider change.

## Become a platform for change

The Best Buy initiative to create the most successful e-waste recycling program in the country (covered in Chapter 2) is one of the most potent examples of becoming a platform for change. The retailer looked beyond its typical products and customer interactions. By installing e-waste recycling bins in every store and doing the hard work of building a supply chain to accept and process used electronics, Best Buy made a significant impact that wasn't ever reflected in its own carbon footprint.

Any business with a customer-facing physical location can do something similar if they choose to do so. Fashion companies can set up bins to accept clothing donations. Grocery stores can (and often do) set up bins to accept canned goods.

But many businesses take the "platform for change" concept even further by working with their customers. The most obvious examples come from the services industry. Marketing agencies may be asked by their clients to come up with a sustainability campaign and suggest some actions to avoid greenwashing claims. Consulting companies have low emissions on their own but can use their customer relationships to help decarbonize other industries. And software companies have an opportunity to use their reach and creativity to move their customers towards more sustainable options.

Navan, formerly known as TripActions, is a corporate travel technology company most recently valued at nearly $10 billion. The business itself doesn't have a particularly high carbon footprint. It's a remotely distributed software company with some business travel and high use of cloud services. Nothing abnormal for a tech company.

But its travel booking platform is part of one of the highest polluting industries in the world. Through the tens of millions of trips booked each year on its platform, Navan's customers are responsible for millions of tons of carbon emissions. Air travel is estimated to account for 20 percent of global emissions, with business travel about 20 percent of that number. So Navan plays a role in enabling a process that contributes 4–5 percent of the world's total emissions.

And yet, the company has no responsibility to act on this. It has a business to run, and business travel is important to its customers. If business travel went away for the sake of the climate, the many people who support the industry, including the almost 2,000 people employed at Navan, would lose their jobs. And business travel isn't going away. If anything, it is increasing at a faster rate post-pandemic than anyone would expect. Plus, from a sustainability perspective, if Navan helped reduce its customers' emissions, that wouldn't reflect on its own carbon footprint. When I use Navan to buy a flight to a conference, those emissions are reflected in my company's carbon accounting, not Navan's. Reducing my travel emissions wouldn't directly help Navan from a business or sustainability angle.

But its sustainability team, nicknamed Tree Actions as a reference to their original company name, saw an opportunity to make a difference anyway. Navan introduced multiple products that helped business travelers make more sustainable decisions. The first, in 2019, was a tool to help companies understand their corporate travel footprint. Companies who book their travel through Navan can get a clear picture of the emissions generated by their employees' travel. As Navan's CEO Ariel Cohen told me:

"Our responsibility is to show you what you are emitting and give you choices to improve your habits in ways that make a difference." They weren't going to push their customers to make new decisions, just provide the information that might lead companies to make different choices.

"And sure," Cohen continued, "a company might take that emissions data and put it into an ESG report and feel good that they've started to measure. But some companies, and some travelers, might use this information to actually change their choices. And we can help them make those new decisions, if they want to."

Navan's next product recommended more sustainable travel options if available. This product was particularly successful in Europe, where rail is pervasive. When a customer went on Navan to book a flight, the platform would show a similar route via train and display any time-inconvenience and emissions savings. "Looking for a flight from London to Paris? Here are your options. And just in case you're curious, you can also take this train. It will cost $50 less, take 25 minutes longer, and save 97 percent emissions." This nudge followed the customer throughout the booking experience but was never in the way. If a customer chose to fly, it was Navan's job to make that booking as seamless as possible. But Navan also knew that its customers might want the win-win outcome of choosing more sustainable options. As Ariel Cohen described his thinking to me:

"Everything at Navan is about win-win. The company gets something, but the employees can participate too. If the traveler chooses a route that emits less carbon, that's good for the company's carbon footprint and the employee should be rewarded. In Navan, we let companies set a carbon budget – the amount of $CO_2$ emissions they don't want to exceed. If employees choose more sustainable travel options, they can earn points and rewards. We're not going to tell you not to book that flight. We're just going to give you the choice. Just offering that choice led to a major reduction in carbon emissions booked through our platform. In Europe, travelers started choosing the lower-emissions route 18 percent more often once we made it easy and shared the data."

Navan didn't browbeat customers with their values of sustainability. It just used its strengths – intuitive software design and strong data – to make sustainability a good business decision. They became a platform for change.

In a particularly interesting example from an ethics perspective, one of the world's leaders in corporate sustainability is using its customer relationships to push for change in one of the world's dirtiest industries.

Microsoft is one of the loudest voices in corporate sustainability. It has dozens of people working full-time in sustainability, ambitious net-zero claims, has been powered by renewable energy for years, and is as committed to sustainable action and transparency as any other tech company.

But the company makes millions in revenue selling software to oil and gas companies. Microsoft even published a press release in 2019 in which it proudly announced that its technology would help ExxonMobil increase oil production by 50,000 barrels/day.

Does that make Microsoft's leaders hypocrites, because you can't wave your hands and yell sustainability while expanding oil production?

Are they capitalists, because their job is increasing the stock price? Complaining about the source of a significant amount of revenue would be fiscally irresponsible.

Are they 3D chess players, because they can fix the system from the inside and help move oil and gas companies towards renewables?

Or are they realists? Some would say that sustainability isn't black and white, and Microsoft should be allowed to make genuine strides to reduce emissions in some parts of its business while making a lot of money from oil and gas companies. This helps people keep the lights and heat on whilst renewables are still a small part of the energy economy.

In an interview for *Protocol*, Microsoft President Brad Smith commented on the relationship between Microsoft and the oil giants. He said that Microsoft's policy was to help these companies transition to clean fuels and a net-zero economy and make them successful in the new green economy.

"We shouldn't want them to die. In my opinion, I think we should want them to transform. And you don't help people transform if you stop working with them."

In other words, Microsoft intends to be a platform for change for its customers. The company wants to be at the table with its customers and push them – through tools, policies, and relationships – to transition to a more sustainable economy. Microsoft knows that fossil fuel companies can get software somewhere else. If Microsoft fired Exxon as a customer, it might be annoying for a bit but Exxon would stumble for a week, then find a similar service from a Microsoft competitor with a lower moral standard. By continuing to work with fossil fuel customers, Microsoft believes it can push customers towards change more quickly.

However, Microsoft employees might feel more conflicted about these relationships than their leaders do. When I posed this question on LinkedIn, a Microsoft employee responded:

"As an employee of Microsoft who has brought this issue up internally with company leadership, it's a salient question – arguably the most important one our company and the broader tech sector will have to grapple with this decade as sustainability increases in importance and climate change ravages the planet with increasing ferocity. I suspect most companies will say they can do both at the same time: work with the fossil fuel companies of today to make their business more 'efficient' and 'profitable' while having a seat at the table to 'help them transition to become the energy companies of the future.' Sounds nice of course, but so far, all evidence points to platitudes and empty gestures."

Becoming a platform for change by helping your customers make more sustainable decisions is one of the most difficult and rewarding jobs of a sustainability team. Whether you're serving salads to city slickers or software and services to businesses, help your customers find opportunities for decarbonization. Give them the tools and knowledge to make more sustainable decisions and reduce their emissions. If you do it well, your own sustainability program will increase in relevance and the topic of sustainability will be at the forefront of our entire economy.

But, as the passionate Microsoft employee shows clearly, a good sustainability program has one final stakeholder to engage in emissions reduction efforts. Employees are your most passionate champions and honest critics. Let's explore how to involve them in your sustainability work early and often.

## EMPLOYEES

Inspiring change among employees is one of the most effective levers for a sustainability leader. Not only are there tangible ways to reduce emissions in your company's carbon accounting, but you'll be able to inspire emissions reduction outside of the workplace while building a convincing case for the importance of your work at the company.

Employees, especially employees under the age of forty, are looking for inspiration in their work. No matter what their company builds as its core product or service, they want to find an employer aligned with their own personal values.

According to the *Cone Communications Millennial Employee Engagement Study*, "64 percent of Millennials consider a company's social and environmental commitments when deciding where to work, 64 percent won't take a job if a company doesn't have strong corporate social responsibility (CSR) values, 83 percent would be more loyal to a company that helps them contribute to social and environmental issues (vs. 70 percent U.S. average), and 88 percent say their job is more fulfilling when they are provided opportunities to make a positive impact on social and environmental issues."

That's why sustainability programs often begin in the human resources and people department. Employees are among the first stakeholders to be brought into a sustainability effort as the ones doing the work to make the business more sustainable. Many programs begin because just a few important employees are loud about wanting their company to take action. It's always better to start promoting internally – where you can test messaging and avoid greenwashing accusations – before beginning your promotion outside the company.

There are three ways to think about working with your employees around sustainability: education, at-work emissions reduction, and out-of-work emissions reduction. Let's go through them one at a time.

## Climate education

Sometimes, the most impactful thing that your sustainability team can do doesn't actually help to lower your company's carbon footprint. Climate education falls squarely into that category. It is an important part of a corporate sustainability program. It builds employee engagement, which shows ROI. It is good for the climate. But it will not directly lower your carbon footprint at all.

And yet, you should still do it.

Climate education is about teaching the people who work for your company about what is happening in climate change. It can involve how to reduce their carbon emissions – which we will talk about in the next two sections – but is just as often about general education around the goals and challenges.

Instead of thinking up novel ideas that have a climate tilt, use existing channels to bring up climate change. For example, Mexican restaurant group bartaco started including a sustainability section in every employee newsletter. Microsoft often hosts fireside chats and invites speakers from the leading edge of climate science. Pinterest organizes beach clean-ups as volunteering opportunities.

Teaching your employees to see the impacts of, and solutions to, human-caused climate change everywhere they go will help bring more people into the fight and result in new behaviors in personal and professional lives to help reduce emissions.

## In-office emissions

Remember that one of your core goals, and what your company will measure your success by, is your ability to reduce the company's total carbon footprint (or at least its carbon intensity). So it's important to find ways to work with your employees to help them reduce their at-work footprint.

Inspiring your employees to reduce waste and change habits will allow your business to reduce emissions from purchased goods (Scope 3, Category 1) while saving money for the company. One of my favorite anecdotes comes from a large law firm that had a printer in every lawyer's office. One weekend, when everyone was out, the IT staff removed the printers from every single office. This change made it much less convenient for a lawyer to print documents. Instead of printing everything simply because it was easy, albeit unnecessary, they now had to walk down a long hallway to a centrally located printer. This meant that printing became both an inconvenience and something noticed (and possibly frowned upon) by peers who would watch you do your printer walk of shame. This one change significantly reduced the amount of paper the law firm needed to purchase, saving money and reducing the company's carbon footprint.

You can also reduce your company's Scope 3, Category 1 footprint by focusing on the food you make available to your employees. Most modern companies have snacks and drinks around the office and often buy their employees lunch or dinner. Take a look at your snack purchases and consider replacing less environmentally friendly options (like beef jerky) or single-wrapped items (like individual bags of chips or plastic water bottles) with vegan or vegetarian options in bulk containers.

Reducing energy use through certain habit changes is a common strategy, but can be more attractive in theory than practice. Putting someone in charge of unplugging monitors and turning off lights every night and weekend is a great idea to reduce emissions, but these habit-based energy savings are not going to be very significant. If your office has one 1,000 square foot room where the lights remain on 24/7 (instead of just 10 hours/day), that can amount to about 2,000 kWh of wasted energy each year, or about 0.75 mt of $CO_2e$ at a cost of $300 (at rates of $0.16 per kWh). While every little bit counts, it's not a significant savings in carbon emissions or money when a 250-person software company might have a total footprint of thousands of metric tons.

This doesn't mean you should leave the lights on all weekend, or that assigning someone to unplug unused devices is a bad idea. At the very least, it educates employees about responsible energy practices that they may take into their own lives while saving the company a little bit of money. And it's a free effort that sends a strong message about wasting less. Even though every effort counts, you should be aware of the impact of different initiatives, so you can focus on the most important ones.

Once you've made a plan to reduce emissions in the office, it's time to look at how employees get to work.

## Out-of-office emissions – commute

All companies, whether or not they require in-person work, have employee commute as part of their carbon footprint. That's because, according to the GHG Protocol, if a company chooses to measure emissions from work-from-home, it would fall under the "employee commute" category (Scope 3, Category 7.)

So as you think about employee commute, your approach to employees who actually leave their homes to go to work, and to those who work out of their homes, is different.

For those with a physical commute, your effort might start with a clean commute policy. In this policy, you lay out your preference for, and plan to enable, greener commuting options. It's like an exercise in vision boarding, where you'll list all the things you'll want to do for your commuting emissions. But as a formal policy, it has the added benefit of needing a signature and buy-in from an executive. Once something is formalized as a policy it has real power, instead of just being a nice-to-have effort from a well-meaning HR team.

While advice is always difficult to generalize, it is particularly challenging in this category. Reducing emissions from employee commute requires different initiatives depending on whether your employees are in cities or more suburban or rural areas. Even if they are in cities, where public transportation is more accessible, different cities and different neighborhoods within cities have different availability and quality of public transit.

It is challenging to come up with solutions without knowing how many of your employees own cars, use cars to get to work, and their proximity to other employees for carpools. Not to mention the cars they drive – a Prius obviously has different emissions than the stretch Hummer that Tony from accounting bought unironically in 2003 and hasn't been able to sell.

So the first step, no matter what kind of business you're in, is an employee commute survey. This is often conducted in the carbon accounting process, as it is the only way to really understand how your employees are commuting these days. You'll ask questions like, "How often do you commute to the office?" and "When you commute, what mode of transportation do you take?" and "How many square feet is your home office?" All of these are meant to provide the company with primary data to understand emissions from Scope 3, Category 7, employee commute. (Remember that work-from-home emissions are covered under this category too.) Once you have a baseline understanding of your employees' commuting habits and emissions, you can begin to consider which option is best for your employees.

Many companies choose to make public transit a more desirable option. Stripe, the payments technology company, provides a monthly reimbursement for public transit as a benefit. This makes the decision to take the subway or bus to work, instead of a private car, the preferred option.

Other companies with employees in urban cities with safe bike lanes might incentivize non-car transportation. Startups like Ride Panda work with companies like Amazon and Intuit to make it easy to offer employees e-bikes and electric scooters as a benefit to encourage employees to skip the car.

Some companies offer subsidies. Apex, an energy company based in Virginia, offers $4,000 off the cost of purchasing an electric vehicle. This is a substantial investment not available to most companies. But it shows a strong commitment to values and acts as an inspiring employee perk. It would certainly attract some employees much more than a welcome basket with branded sweatshirts and water bottles or a chocolate-making class.

If your employees work from home, the biggest changes you can make are to help reduce the emissions of your employees' homes. Because work-from-home emissions are calculated by multiplying the amount of energy used for a forty-hour workweek by the square footage of a typical home office (and a few emissions factors), the obvious way to reduce that number is to help your employees reduce energy use in their houses.

Start with what's free. Remind your employees to turn off lights in rooms that are unused and unplug monitors and unused appliances overnight and on weekends away. This education costs your business nothing and will help your employees save money.

If the budget is available and your employees are interested, you can offer to subsidize more substantial changes. Predominantly, that involves the switch to renewable energy (often by paying the difference for any opt-in renewable energy program that your employees' utility provider might offer) or incentivizing more infrastructural changes like the installation of solar panels or heat pumps. This takes more effort and budget, as you should research the best way to do this on behalf of your employees and come up with the programs and funding to reimburse part of these costs.

In addition to employee commute, employees also directly impact business travel (Scope 3, Category 6 in the GHG Protocol).

## Out-of-office emissions – business travel

Business travel is (almost) back. The industry reached a 2019 peak in terms of number of travelers and total spend before plummeting during the COVID pandemic. But while the shift to remote work and the option for multi-million dollar Zoom deals is a trend, not a fad, business travel remains important.

Sustainability teams cannot, and perhaps should not, fight this trend too hard. Yes, it's true that travel accounts for about 8 percent of global emissions, with transport (airplanes, cars, and ships) making up about half of that total. And yes, it's true that one of the biggest contributors to a corporate carbon footprint is business travel. And yes, it's true that many businesses can run adequately behind Zoom screens.

But it is also true that, putting sustainability aside for a moment, people want to get back together. Conferences are back to near pre-pandemic popularity. Managers want to bring teams, which scattered around the world during COVID, together in person for bonding, brainstorming, and working. Whether business travel is pitched as necessary for business (sales happen in person!) or culture (we're more creative at our corporate ski trip / annual planning meeting!), business travel is often just plain fun. Going on paid trips to cool places is one of the perks of working for a large company. Sustainability programs will not succeed if they go counter to what people want to do. You can't be the only employee who refuses to travel, and you can't pester your colleagues with reminders about the climate effects of flying. They don't want to hear it and will quickly cut you out.

Instead, you can make changes to how your business does corporate travel that are in line with how the leaders want to operate.

A sustainable travel policy promotes a more responsible, low-emissions form of travel and has a few key components:

- Requires use of an emissions estimator, like Google Flights or Navan, to choose flights with lower carbon emissions
- Restricts commuter flights, or flights under 60–90 minutes, when travel by train or vehicle is available
- When renting a car, encourages renting electric vehicles over gas
- Everyone below Vice President level needs approval for all travel
- Sales can only travel for over $50,000 in opportunity. Anything less requires VP approval

Visit attainablesustainabilitybook.com/travel for a free sustainable travel policy template.

The best inhibitor to travel is the adoption of technology and smart local planning. If your team feels like they can have productive relationships over Zoom, Teams, Slack, and Virtual Reality (if that's still a thing as you read this) then they might put off a trip. If members of teams that work together are based in the same offices, there will be fewer reasons to travel.

If travel is a core part of your carbon emissions and an area you want to focus on, start moving money towards decarbonizing this emissions-intensive industry. The most important developments in aviation will be cleaner jet fuel and, further in the future, electric or hydrogen-powered planes. Consider moving a small amount of capital to fund that research as part of your sustainability strategy.

One suggestion introduced to me by the sustainability team of a forward-thinking technology company is to impose an internal carbon tax on travel. The US EPA has a current carbon tax of $51/ton and is considering raising it to $190/ton. This is what they consider to be the "social cost of carbon," or the effect that one ton of carbon will have on society. Your company can take these numbers as markers and impose an internal social cost of carbon on all business travel.

You'll then set a carbon budget for your company total (i.e., "We won't exceed 2,000 mt $CO_2$e from flights each quarter") and divide that budget up by team (i.e., "Sales won't exceed 500 mt per quarter, HR won't exceed 100 mt per quarter"). Your sustainability software partner can help you keep live tabs on how travel is affecting emissions.

Whenever a team exceeds its travel emissions budget, its manager must earmark funds to pay for the internal cost of carbon (i.e., "Sales travel emissions were 600 mt last quarter, they need to pay a tax on that 100 mt excess at our company's internal cost of carbon of $51/ton"). That money will go to the sustainability team to spend on initiatives like sponsoring cleaner jet fuel. Your managers' budget won't change, so they will either need to learn to travel less (great for emissions reduction!) or request more money to pay for this carbon tax (great for investment in clean jet fuel).

This isn't an easy program to build out and requires a lot of sign-off. But if you want to align the entire company towards your climate goals, you'll need to set up an incentive system that gets everyone moving in the same direction.

Now, while all of the above will impact your Scope 3 emissions, one of your biggest opportunities for emissions lies in Scope 2, or energy.

## ENERGY

Energy is such an important part of a company's carbon footprint that it gets its own Scope in the GHG Protocol (Scope 2). There are three things you can do to reduce your emissions around energy: your company can reduce how much energy you consume, switch fully to renewable energy, and support the growth of renewable energy options by purchasing renewable energy credits. Let's explore these one at a time.

### Reduce energy consumption

Reduction always comes first. Clean energy is great. Solar power is definitely cleaner than its oil and gas counterparts, but it still takes materials to produce and generates a certain amount of waste. So while you should switch to renewable energy as quickly and completely as possible, as we'll explore in the next two sections, reducing your total energy use should be the primary goal.

Your first strategy should be upgrading existing appliances to energy-efficient alternatives. This can have a significant impact on your energy emissions. Appliances that have earned the Energy Star certification, designed and managed by the US Environmental Protection Agency, can be 10–35 percent more efficient than their older, less-clean counterparts. This improvement shows itself with measurably reduced energy use and translates into real savings.

For example, a restaurant using an Energy Star-rated electric griddle instead of an old griddle can save 11 percent more energy, which can amount to over $1,000 on utility bills over the product's lifetime.

While replacing an appliance can cost a business real money, the government wants to support the transition to a clean energy economy by providing tax deductions to subsidize these investments. If you work at a restaurant with many appliances, or even a software or services business with a full kitchen, ask your accounting team to look into the Section 179D Tax Deduction. This tax clause offers companies a tax deduction of up to $1.80 per square foot for qualifying investments.

You can also reduce emissions by changing employee and customer habits. Your business uses energy twenty-four hours/day. Lights are on, air conditioning is running, and computers are plugged in. All of these draw power from the grid and contribute to your utility bill. While your energy use will never go down to absolute zero, new habits from your employees and customers can reduce the energy used.

If yours is a location-based business with dozens of similar concepts across the country, you have a special opportunity to find insights that lead to less energy use and more profit. Find software that can extract data from your utility bills in a live view and feed you insights as to your best- and worst-performing locations, normalized per square foot. You'll quickly see that your least efficient locations may be spending up to eight times more money per square foot on energy. You'll have to do some work to diagnose the issue, but just seeing the data update live, in one view, will show you opportunities for big savings.

I saw this data uncover a variety of issues across restaurants. One health food chain with sixty locations noticed that it was paying the utility bills for its neighbor, which reflected poorly on its carbon footprint. One wine bar with twenty-one locations saw that a poorly designed event space attached to the main restaurant forced the air conditioning and heater to work twice as hard as needed and put in a cheap, thin wall that saved the company hundreds of dollars per month. One Mexican restaurant with 40 locations saw that bad habits like leaving the door open on a hot day or turning on a backup oven first thing in the morning meant that identical concepts could be spending twice as much as their peers in the same city.

Hilton Hotels developed LightStay, an energy tracking system that led to a 6.6 percent reduction in energy use and over $74 million in savings. It took this data further and began to engage customers in its sustainability efforts, a system replicated by most hotels. Hotels ask customers to opt-in for room service and towel washing, which saves energy and water usage. Hotels often install lights that require a key card to work. If the customer leaves and takes their key card, lights around the room will turn off even if the customer forgot to flip the switch.

Laundromats create habit-change in their customers by reducing the cost of service at times when energy is cheaper. The energy grid is under its most pressure – and at its highest cost – in the middle of the day. Laundry companies now incentivize customers to use their services early in the morning or late at night to reduce the load on the energy grid, save costs, and lower emissions.

While you'll always use energy, switching to renewable energy is one of the biggest changes your company needs to make.

## Switch to renewable energy

Some companies, by virtue of luck or planning, operate in geographies powered by renewable energy. In 2022, about 50 percent of energy generated in California came from renewables (and in 2023 they reached 100 percent renewable power for stretches of a few hours). Certain countries (Sweden, Iceland, Uruguay, Costa Rica) have been investing in renewable energy for decades and have 98 percent of their power coming from renewable energy sources. But if luck, foresight, and policy didn't come together to power your buildings with renewable energy, there are two ways to begin your switch.

The first route is to build your own clean energy generators. If you own your buildings, you can install solar panels. With enough planning and will, you can start a coalition of local companies to combine capital and build out a solar or wind farm from which your businesses can draw power.

Fast food chain KFC recently installed solar panels over the canopy in its drive-through in Bakersfield, California, and found multiple benefits. The marketing was amazing, as local news came to do ribbon cuttings and the drive-through was featured in dozens of industry publications.

The business is also going to see a strong financial return. As reported in *thetakeout.com*:

*"...the owners soon realized that, thanks to tax credits on solar panels, they could install a solar-powered canopy and recover the cost within five years. The 72-foot canopy, designed by Integrate Solar, contains 57 solar panels. Although the cost of the panels was not disclosed, the new canopy is expected to save the restaurant $11,000 in energy costs in just its first year, and $400,000 over its lifetime."*

To install your own solar panels, you'll need the right financing, the support of your landlord, and a very long-term view on that piece of real estate. When the stars don't align for a direct switch to renewable energy, companies in certain geographies have an indirect option.

Community solar allows a group of people and businesses to "lease" part of a solar array and use the energy themselves. To do this, you can reach out to your local utility and see if there are available community solar programs near your offices for you to join. If not, you can take the lead by bringing together businesses from your area to support the build out of a community solar farm.

This is a high-impact, direct way to put money into moving the grid towards renewable energy. It may require a significant upfront investment, but with proper financing and tax credits, it could also help your business save a significant amount of money on utilities over the course of a few years.

The rules for community solar vary per state, as only one-third of states have passed formal legislation around the program. The best way to explore if this project makes sense for your business is to reach out directly to your utility company.

If none of these options are available, renewable energy credits are your next best solution.

## Purchase renewable energy credits

A renewable energy credit, or REC, is a financial tool to signal to utility companies around the world that there is serious interest in purchasing renewable energy. It tells the market that if they invested the heavy upfront costs of building the windmills and solar farms needed to supply the world with clean, renewable electricity, the world would happily pay for it. RECs are best used by companies for whom switching to renewable energy is not a viable option.

When you purchase RECs, you are supporting the creation of as much clean energy as you used in your reporting year. So if your company calculates that your offices used 1,000 MWh of energy in the 12-month period you are reporting in, you can purchase 1,000 MWh of RECs in addition to what you've already paid your utility.

You are spending money the utility company wouldn't have otherwise received, and sending the energy markets a strong demand signal to build more renewables. They know that if they invest in solar and wind energy, the buyers will be there waiting. This helps utilities bring down the cost of renewable energy and is a tangible way for the business community to support investments in an important decarbonization effort.

When you purchase quality RECs, you get added business benefits.

According to the GHG Protocol, you can apply the purchase of RECs against market-based energy emissions in Scope 2. This will help you claim reduced Scope 2 emissions when you report on your aggregate carbon footprint.

If purchasing RECs, you will need to report both location-based and market-based Scope 2 emissions. Location-based emissions are the actual emissions from your buildings without applying renewable energy credits. Market-based emissions apply RECs to come up with a reduced number. Technology company Okta does this well in its FY22 GHG emissions report (table 4.1).

**Okta FY22 Emissions**

| Emissions | FY20 tCO2e | FY20 % of total | FY21 tCO2e | FY21 % of total | FY22 tCO2e | FY22 % of total | Change from FY21 to FY22 % of total |
|---|---|---|---|---|---|---|---|
| Scope 1 | 0 | 0% | 0 | 0% | 0 | 0% | 0% |
| Scope 2 Location Based | 1,411 | - | 1,340 | - | 1,469 | - | 10% |
| Scope 2 Market Based | 1,103 | 3% | 658 | 2% | 254 | <1% | -61% |
| Scope 3 | 37,404 | 97% | 35,237 | 98% | 55,589 | >99% | 58% |
| Total Market based | 38,508 | - | 35,895 | - | 55,843 | - | 56% |

Source: Okta 2022 GHG Emissions Report https://www.okta.com/sites/default/files/2022-10/FY22-Okta-GHG-Emissions.pdf

Table 4.1. Okta reduced its reported emissions with RECs

Another benefit of using RECs is permission to tell the market that you are "Powered by Renewable Energy," which sends a strong marketing message to customers, employees, and investors that sustainability matters and that you are putting your money where your mouth is.

Starbucks uses renewable energy credits to make the claim that its stores are "powered by sunshine." Since 2015, the company has purchased enough RECs to power 100 percent of its more than 9,000 company-operated stores in the U.S. and Canada with clean energy.

In 2017, the company spent over $70 million on renewable energy credits, but it took over a decade to get there. It describes the process in a 2018 blog post:

"Starbucks' commitment to renewable energy has increased since 2005, a year after the company undertook its first-ever inventory of its own greenhouse gas emissions. That analysis revealed that 70 percent of emissions came from the purchase of electricity to power stores. 'Starbucks takes its role as a responsible corporation seriously,' said Rebecca Zimmer, the company's director of global environmental impact. 'We understand one of the largest areas of responsibility involves the emissions from electricity generation, which contribute to climate change that puts our business and the communities in which we operate at risk.'

Starbucks began by purchasing 5 percent renewable energy in 2005; within a decade, it was purchasing a kilowatt of renewable 'green' energy for every kilowatt of 'brown' electricity used – traditional fossil fuel-based energy such as coal and natural gas."

Starbucks, a company with a dedicated and sophisticated sustainability department, realized that renewable energy credits were its fastest and most direct path to making claims of being powered by renewables and to pushing utility providers to build out bigger renewable projects.

Ben & Jerry's is an interesting example of a company that built its own solar panels but still purchases RECs to support its claim of being powered by renewable energy. In 2016, the company built a small solar farm near its corporate HQ that produces 0.74 MWh of clean energy. While certainly a worthy investment, 0.74 MWh is enough to power a single Ben & Jerry's ice cream shop for a few hours. That's a few hundred Americone Dreams at best.

But the company still proudly boasts that it is powered by renewable energy. It does this by purchasing RECs to subsidize its inability to draw enough actual clean energy from the grid. And the company is transparent about this in its annual sustainability reports, writing (in its 2020 report):

*"Unilever North America [Ben & Jerry's corporate owner] procures Green-e RECs for electricity (Scope 2) on a national scale from solar and wind sources and has been procuring these RECs for 100 percent of electricity usage on behalf of Ben & Jerry's since 2011. These North America RECs cover electricity usage from manufacturing, offices, company-owned scoop shops, and distribution centers in the US and Canada. Unilever Europe procures power purchase agreements and 'guarantee of origin' RECs for electricity from wind sources and has been procuring electricity RECs for the majority of electricity usage on behalf of Ben & Jerry's since 2011."*

Your company is unlikely to build its own solar farm. You would need to own the property, put together the capital, and spend the time and resources to do it. Even if you had all of those things set up and were a loud and proud sustainability brand, like Ben & Jerry's, your efforts might still create too small an amount of energy. The benefit of doing it is not some massive contribution to a cleaner grid; it is in the statement and the marketing benefit associated with this effort. Putting your name and dollars behind a project like building your own solar panels or wind farms signifies a serious commitment to clean energy and may inspire others.

The most beneficial impact your company can have is pushing the broader system to change. It should be utility companies and power plant operators that drive the move to renewable energy from a manufacturing perspective, not scattered individual companies. Building solar panels is fantastic, as every addition to the clean energy future is meaningful in both pure energy and market education terms, but driving dollars towards renewables at scale via RECs has a much more potent impact.

Reducing emissions rarely happens in a vacuum. Great sustainability programs engage suppliers, customers, and employees and find ways to reduce carbon emissions across their entire ecosystem.

Energy is such a large contributor to carbon emissions that it gets its own Scope – Scope 2 – in carbon accounting. To make a difference, find ways to reduce consumption, switch to renewable energy, and leverage renewable energy credits.

Once you have reduced your emissions, you will need to communicate your corporate sustainability program. Large companies will be required to report on sustainability progress, while all customers deserve to market their accomplishments. Building your communication strategy is the subject of the next chapter.

## SUMMARY

- Great sustainability programs engage suppliers, customers, and employees to reduce internal and external emissions.
- Energy is such a large contributor to carbon emissions that it gets its own Scope in carbon accounting.
- Tackle energy use by reducing consumption, switching to renewable energy, and leveraging renewable energy credits.

## ACTIONS

Look at what you learned in the carbon accounting process. Find some low-hanging fruit, or carbon reduction efforts that have a high chance of being implemented quickly, even if they won't reduce emissions by a lot. Quick wins will build momentum for your sustainability program.

Balance that with 1–2 long-term efforts that will take a lot of time or cost a lot of money. Begin building a plan and gaining support for those more difficult strategies.

Don't take on more than you can handle, and don't overcommit. Start small, engage stakeholders, and build towards big goals over time.

*Chapter 5*

# COMMUNICATE

Your sustainability program is at the center of a small gear; one part of the massive machine that is the fight against climate change. From your center emerge many spokes – all of the stakeholders who interact with your company and your product. And they, in turn, press up against other gears: pushing, pressuring, and turning them to make the full anti-climate change machine turn. Telling your stakeholders about your sustainability work, explaining the importance of this effort, and teaching them how to make their own improvements can have powerful impacts down the line.

Sustainability communication takes two forms. The first is required reporting to regulators, investors, and customers. The second is voluntary communication (aka marketing) to customers and employees. Some companies start working and communicating on sustainability voluntarily, as part of a core value or recognition of the brand benefits. Others wait until reporting is required. No matter how committed your company is to sustainability, you'll need to figure out a communication strategy that both earns an ROI and keeps you out of trouble.

What many companies often fear, and rightfully so, is being slapped with a greenwashing label. The concern is a real one, as it results in bad press, a hit to the brand, and reduced faith in corporate sustainability efforts. In still rare but increasingly common cases, companies can even be fined for being misleading in their communications.

In this chapter, we'll look at what greenwashing really means and how to avoid it, and how to formulate a strategy to communicate your efforts to employees, customers, and investors. Finally, we'll examine the most popular climate frameworks companies can submit to.

Once your company has done the hard work of taking action to reduce your emissions and has set up the infrastructure for transparency, you can begin to confidently market your work. If done well, marketing will create real business opportunities. If mismanaged, you will be accused of greenwashing.

We've mentioned greenwashing a few times in this book already. Now, as we explore marketing in depth, it's time to build a true understanding of the term. You cannot avoid something unless you know how to define it, so let's start there.

The fancy definition of greenwashing reads something like:

"Greenwashing is a marketing technique that involves using environmental buzzwords, symbols, or imagery in advertising, packaging, or promotion to create the impression of environmental responsibility, while downplaying or ignoring negative environmental impacts."

A simpler way to say it is, "Greenwashing is making sustainability claims before you've earned the right to do so."

Of course, there is nothing wrong with promoting your sustainability efforts and marketing yourself as a more climate-friendly option. When done properly, that's the kind of marketing that changes buying habits, educates markets, and inspires political action.

Good sustainability marketing can educate, inspire, and excite your customers. Your marketing team can help people reduce waste, support important causes, and feel proud about the decisions they make. Sustainability marketing, which helps elevate climate to the top of the national conversation, is as important a tool as any other in the transition to a green economy.

The issue arises when this marketing makes undeserved claims that lack one or both tenets of good sustainability communication. Marketing without first taking action is asking for unearned credit. Marketing without transparency is demanding unearned trust.

The most egregious of these claims comes from high-polluting industries waving their arms around screaming "We're sustainable!" while delaying significant action and using inaccurate data to back up preposterous claims.

The European airline Ryanair faced this exact challenge in 2020. The year prior, Ryanair was the first non-coal company to be named on the European Union's highest-emitter list. In addressing this dubious honor, the marketing team was tasked with rebranding the company as sustainable. This could have been the company's chance to build a plan to decarbonize the airline industry by measuring emissions, investing in renewable fuels, and reducing waste on planes.

Instead of doing the hard work, though, the company ran an advertising campaign claiming to have the lowest carbon emissions of any major airline. Ryanair argued that because it had newer airplanes and a higher percentage of seats filled, it must be a more sustainable airline.

No action. No transparency. Just claims and promises. That's what got the company into trouble with the UK's Advertising

Standards Authority. The company was forced to retract the entire campaign, costing it millions of dollars.

While it's understandable that companies from high-emitting industries like airlines or oil and gas can be accused of greenwashing, the same also happens in less carbon-intensive businesses. In 2020, the restaurant-rating guide Michelin debuted a green clover icon to recognize restaurants making advances in reducing food waste and energy consumption. Sounds like a nice thought, doesn't it?

Michelin awarded one of the first green clovers to chef Christian Puglisi of Danish restaurant Relae. But instead of taking the honor and stamping it on every menu and Instagram post, the chef decided to raise a complaint. He believed that a sustainability claim deserved a lot more scrutiny and was honest about his own restaurant's climate issues, from using a lot of power for heat in the winter to serving meat.

Puglisi went to the press with his opinion that Michelin did minimal due diligence to find sustainable champions. "If the Michelin Guide wants to do something about sustainability, then they need to challenge us. They need to make an effort in trying to make us make an effort. We need gastronomy to wake up and put the money where its mouth is." In other words, he wanted Michelin to take action and show transparency around its work.

Chef Puglisi's statements created dozens of articles with negative press for Michelin's new green clover award, proving that just making claims around sustainability without doing the hard work of decarbonizing isn't going to cut it.

Greenwashing hurts companies with fines, wasted money, and bad press. Your job, as the executive for sustainability at your company, is to lead your company away from greenwashing. You need to do the hard work to back up your statements. You need to assume that your customers are smart, educated, and passionate.

They want to believe and invest in a cleaner, better world. They want you to be right about everything you are saying.

But they're going to demand quality. They're going to demand research. They're going to demand you spend at least as much time and money on action and transparency in your sustainability work as you do on your sustainability marketing.

## Action and transparency

Some companies, for whom sustainability isn't core to their brand, treat it as little more than a requirement. They don't want to get in trouble for doing it poorly, but they're really only thinking about it because they were made to by an investor, regulator, or important customer. At the opposite end of the spectrum are companies that make sustainability a core part of their business models. They invest money and time into applying best practices to their products, and they've integrated sustainability communication into every customer moment.

It's not unusual to find companies that are hesitant when it comes to telling the world what they're doing. One marketing agency I worked with was told by a large customer to measure its carbon footprint. The agency looked for the easiest way to solve this problem and keep the customer happy. We helped them measure their footprint and report the findings to that customer. Beyond reporting honestly and transparently to any customer requests, the agency's owners simply had no interest in talking about their sustainability work.

A little further along the communication spectrum was a California-based law firm with about 1,300 employees around the country. Its Chief Administrative Officer wanted to build out a sustainability program because it was the right thing to do. It was willing to tell its employees about the work because its employees wanted to see the company do this work. But it insisted it wasn't doing sustainability as a brand-building exercise and had no intention to market its work outside of the company.

While I understand this hesitancy, I don't recommend it to most companies. Even if you don't want to spend much time marketing your efforts, because you are laser-focused on your core business, there are easy ways to make a statement about your work to date and see some ROI from it. And even if you have the philosophy of undertaking sustainability because it's the right thing to do, and not for any marketing benefit, your silence isn't helping to push the sustainability conversation forward in your industry. The right thing to do for the planet would actually be to talk openly about your sustainability work.

Of course, there's the ever-present fear of being labeled a greenwasher. But all companies – even those that don't plan on sustainability being central to the brand – can be role models. They can push their employees and customers to think more about sustainability. They can show regulators that climate change is a problem that corporate America cares deeply about. They can show communities that action is within reach, teach individuals how to be more accountable, and push industry peers to take their own actions. Paying lip service matters.

As you develop your sustainability communication strategy, you should keep two tenets central to your approach: action and transparency.

Action means speaking less about what you want to do than about what you are already doing. Don't start talking about sustainability until you have some very real results to show from internal work. Don't put sustainability as a core value until you've spent the time and money to understand your carbon footprint. Don't spin up a sustainability website until you've made progress reducing your emissions. Don't think you can set a net-zero goal, brag about it in a press release and customer-wide email blast, then put off doing anything until 2040.

Mistaking the order of action and communication has had serious consequences. In February 2023, *The Guardian* reported that sustainability-related advertising from the German airline Lufthansa was going to be banned in the United Kingdom. The ad was an image of a plane with the Earth as its underside and a link to its sustainability website, makechangefly.com. The UK's Advertising Standards Authority launched an investigation that resulted in the banning of the advertisement, in large part because of the forward-looking statements of Lufthansa's sustainability goals.

As the ASA wrote when explaining the ban, "Many of these initiatives are targeted to deliver results only years or decades into the future. We also understood that there were currently no environmental initiatives or commercially viable technologies in the aviation industry which would substantiate the absolute green claim 'protecting its future', as we considered consumers would interpret it."

In other words, Lufthansa claimed to be sustainable just because they'd set some goals. Anyone can set goals. The point – and the hard part – is taking action that makes a meaningful difference.

Action needs to be a core component of your sustainability communication because it is the only thing that the recipient of your comms - be it employees, customers, investors, or partners - can trust. And it needs to be constant. Just because your company started as a sustainable brand doesn't mean your sustainability journey is more complete, or even more credible, than someone else's. Don't forget that no matter what industry you are in, you have an impact on the environment. That's not good or bad, it's just the truth.

For as long as you are in business, you will have opportunities to make new and bigger changes to your company's operations, policies, products, and stakeholder engagement to support the fight against climate change. Sustainability isn't a few boxes to be checked off; it's an infinite staircase. At times, the next step is laid out in front of you. Other times, you've got to search and dig for the best next action. You can never be at the top stair, only a little higher than you were yesterday.

A good example of this is a small gifting company called Loop & Tie. This fifty-person business headquartered in Austin, Texas, was founded in 2013 on the premise that gifting should be less wasteful and more additive to the environment and social ecosystem. It sources gifts from local artisans, invests in fully recyclable and compostable packaging, and offsets double the emissions from every shipment. And it talks about this everywhere, from its website to Instagram to an attachment in every gift it sends.

Loop & Tie does this because it knows it's important to its customers – Fortune 500 companies like Salesforce, Google, and Deloitte – who choose Loop & Tie as their gifting partner because of these sustainability initiatives. And it does it well because it talks about its actions at every point in the road.

As Chief Marketing Officer MK Getler-Porizkova told me in a February 2023 interview, Loop & Tie takes serious action before talking about itself as a sustainable brand. "We are so hesitant to greenwash with anything that we do. We're doing this not because we're looking for something in return. We do this because it's the right way to run a business in today's society. All of our packaging is reusable, recyclable, and biodegradable. We help teach people how to recycle every single tiny aspect of the gift they have received. We offset double the emissions generated from our shipping."

The second key tenet is transparency. The push for transparency started with the investment community searching for a way to value companies consistently. They launched the Task Force for Climate-related Financial Disclosures (TCFD), encouraged companies to submit to the Carbon Disclosure Project (CDP), and asked the SEC to enforce climate disclosures.

Transparency is an expectation of sustainability done well and is an opportunity to build an open and thoughtful relationship with your customers and stakeholders. Without transparency in the work you're doing and the progress you're making, your advertising will seem hollow at best, and misleading at worst.

Keurig, the coffee pod company, felt this pain firsthand. From social media to packaging, Keurig told its Canadian customers that they could recycle their coffee pods. It provided guidance on recycling pods ("just peel the lid and rinse!") and touted its accomplishments as a key sustainability win and a reason to buy Keurig.

Unfortunately, these claims lacked transparency. Only two provinces in all of Canada actually had recycling programs that accepted these pods. And even there, additional steps were often required to make the pod fit for recycling.

Keurig was forced to pay up. Canada's Competition Bureau fined it $3 million, required an $800,000 payment to a Canadian environmental organization, and demanded $85,000 to cover the Bureau's legal costs. The company was forced to change all its packaging and marketing at an unknown (but not small) additional cost, and negative press across dozens of news sites hurt the brand. All of this resulted from an over-eager marketing team and a lack of transparency.

Examples of sustainability communication gone wrong might scare you off doing any marketing around your accomplishments. After all, how do you know if you've taken enough action before communicating? How do you know if you're being transparent enough in what you're communicating? And are you greenwashing? There is a certain line of thinking in the sustainability world that any pride around sustainability should be thought of as greenwashing..

Green packaging on your deodorant? Greenwashing.

Advertisements depicting your product fraternizing with cute chipmunks and planet-conscious centaurs in the forest? Greenwashing.

Idealistic taglines like Lufthansa's "Connecting the world. Protecting its future."? Greenwashing.

There will always be well-meaning groups, from environmental activists to advertising watchdogs, looking to label a brand's communication efforts as greenwashing. It's important work, as brands shouldn't be allowed to make untrue or misleading claims about something as important as sustainability and not pay for their mistakes. An ecosystem of watchdogs will keep the industry honest and accountable and elevate the amount of work a company does before making sustainability claims.

But fear of taking the wrong step shouldn't shut down all sustainability communication. Part of a good sustainability strategy means educating the world about what you are doing. Sustainability needs to be part of the conversation everywhere we go. And, like it or not, marketing is one of the ways that modern companies can see an ROI from the significant investments they are going to be making in sustainability. Companies deserve to see a return on their efforts as it helps them continue to invest more in decarbonization.

Anne-Loure Discours, the Chief Sourcing Officer at the fashion brand PUMA, said it well in an interview with *The Business of Fashion*:

"Nobody is sustainable today. We are all trying to become more sustainable. So what can you communicate? You have to be realistic with what you are really doing. We should be careful not to say 'we are the best' because nobody is the best and nobody is good at that game today. We are all learning, and we are all developing, and we are all trying. It's a constant improvement process. So how you communicate has to remain extremely humble. It's a lot about being extremely humble and extremely transparent."

It is also unfair and unwise to expect companies not to talk about their accomplishments, especially when deserved. So if you're going to communicate about your sustainability work – and you should – remember to always focus on actions over plans, and transparency over big claims.

In this chapter, we'll explore ways of communicating your sustainability efforts to three core constituents – employees, customers, and investors – and look at the most common frameworks for standardized reporting.

## EMPLOYEES

Employee engagement is one of the clearest ROIs most companies will see, and falls under the "voluntary marketing" part of sustainability communication. Chapter 4 went into detail about how to help your employees reduce their emissions. This section is about marketing your climate efforts and progress to employees and new recruits to get them excited about your company. When done well, this will increase retention, support recruiting, and strengthen your sustainability program.

This is true in all businesses. One that's seen great results is the upscale Mexican restaurant bartaco, which has twenty-seven locations. Its climate work and partnership with a carbon accounting software company forms part of every recruiting conversation. CFO Scott Lawton explains:

"One of the more interesting and unanticipated benefits of working with [our carbon accounting partner] has been the overwhelmingly positive reaction from interview candidates when I describe our relationship with [our carbon accounting partner]. This matters, it's part of our culture, and the positive impact it has had on our recruiting has been immeasurable."

It clearly works. But to make sustainability work well as an employee engagement tool, you'll want to have a few things in place.

First, start by finding and mobilizing a group of employees who are already passionate about climate. By getting together a "green team" or a "sustainability employee resource group," you'll give people a formal outlet for commenting on and advancing your business's climate goals. Employees who get involved in the company culture outside of their core work develop deep roots and are less likely to leave. So for employees who want to get involved in climate change but don't feel like they have a way to do that in their normal job, a green team provides an outlet.

Your green team is going to be an important part of your company's sustainability work. They'll be the first employees you communicate your work to, and the first group that will help you champion an emissions reduction strategy. While it may seem like a tiny exercise to establish a green team as part of a corporate sustainability program, many sophisticated programs start in this exact way.

Establishing a green team helps find the internal champions who are the first to want to listen to what your sustainability team has to say. They'll spread the gospel of sustainability through your company, amplifying any message you put out, and providing feedback about what feels authentic and relevant to the brand.

Next, you'll want to start embedding climate into your normal employee communication channels. Many companies spend their day on chat platforms like Slack or Microsoft Teams. Create a #sustainability channel in those platforms. Make it a hub for discussion about climate change news, a place to get people involved in corporate sustainability initiatives, and a medium for sharing the work the company is doing around measuring and reducing its footprint.

You can do the same thing with a newsletter, email list, internal podcast, or intranet page. Wherever your employees go to learn about the happenings of their employer, work with your internal communications to announce the existence of this climate program. You'll find more support than you might expect. Sustainability is a positive effort, and lots of leaders want to be associated with these low-stakes, directional improvements.

What you do with your employees will depend on your internal culture and available resources. Your goal is to get people talking about sustainability, learning about it, and acting in its name in their personal and professional lives. There are many approaches you can take, from organizing volunteering and clean-up events to sharing educational materials and encouraging employees to live more sustainably.

To give you one example, the sales technology company Salesloft participated in the Tiny Climate Acts initiative. Each Earth Month (April), companies participating in the Tiny Climate Acts competition invite employees to upload photos of their small acts of sustainability to a special platform. This might include riding a bike to work, eating a plant-based meal, or unplugging a monitor at night. Each post earns points for the individual and the platform creates an intra-company leaderboard. Companies can reward their best performers with prizes like gift cards to local vegan restaurants, contributions to carbon offset purchases, or a cash bonus.

None of these acts on their own are going to make a huge dent in climate change. But that's not the point. Tiny Climate Acts, and events like it, are meant to inspire people to think about sustainability more often and to build a business case for your company to make more significant contributions.

Salesloft, a company with about 1,000 employees, had over 100 employees submit over 900 Tiny Climate Acts during Earth Month, and rewarded the winner with 500 points on their internal employee rewards program. It used this level of engagement as a proof point in its argument that employees genuinely cared about sustainability and wanted to see the company continue to evolve. The data was presented to executives, along with a request to offset Salesloft's 2022 footprint. The executive team took the strong employee engagement as a sign that further action on climate change could lead to even better business results in the form of improved employee recruitment and retention, and continued its carbon neutrality commitment.

If your green team has the bandwidth, you might want to use these same channels to get employees together for book clubs, webinars, and fireside chats. The climate world is teeming with interesting people. Bringing in a speaker once per quarter to talk about electrification, food waste, or carbon offsets can inspire high employee attendance.

Some programs are fantastic engagement opportunities that help climate education and result in genuine cost savings. Flatiron Health, a New York-based health technology company, decided to host a hackathon focused on sustainability. Over seventy employees across the company participated in a three-day event, searching for ideas to reduce the company's carbon footprint and improve its contributions to a net-zero economy.

The engineering team, a group of individuals with no background in sustainability, stumbled upon a solution that only an engineering team would ever find. The team realized that due to a mix of unneeded and mismanaged data, the company was likely using a lot more Amazon Web Services resources than it required.

Through a mix of engineering changes and management and behavioral adjustments, the team was able to save over $1,000,000 on its annual AWS bill. The team felt validated in their work, the company got to report a year-over-year reduction in emissions, the CFO was thrilled to find savings, the CEO got to post something exciting on LinkedIn… it was a true win-win. To read the rest of this story and learn how to set up a climate hackathon of your own, search for "Flatiron health sustainability hackathon" on LinkedIn.

Getting employees excited about your work is going to be one of the easiest, lowest-cost ways to derive an ROI from your sustainability work. Once your employees start to see the company as a brand that cares about climate, they will stay longer and find their work more rewarding.

It's always good to start sustainability work internally to get employees aligned and make sure you're taking action before communicating externally. Eventually, however, you're going to need to start to share your sustainability data and story with customers.

## CUSTOMERS

If you serve an enterprise customer, your sustainability program might be kicked off by required reporting. As we've explored previously in this book, companies are starting to demand that their largest suppliers report on carbon emissions and reduction strategies, which means you'll need to empower your sales team to answer all incoming questions.

But smart sustainability teams will also see opportunities to integrate climate into the marketing strategy of the company. The visibility will help cement the importance of your work.

Customer marketing can be divided into two layers: brand marketing is high-level storytelling that establishes your company's identity as a sustainable brand, while action-based marketing engages your customers with useful or interesting content whenever they interact with your products.

### Brand marketing

Brands that are seen as sustainable make customers feel better about their buying decisions. If the sustainability efforts are genuine and effective, such brands can command a premium price.

One of your first steps, then, is to build a sustainability page on your website. You can see this page near the "about us" section of most websites, as companies try to establish their sustainability brands and explain their approach to climate.

As you think about your sustainability brand, you'll want to think about the same approaches that led you away from greenwashing – action and transparency. Talk about what you are already doing much more than what you plan on doing. Show numbers wherever possible. Don't shy away from explaining what you don't yet know about your carbon footprint or what is left to do to reduce emissions.

This page should not have to change frequently. You may want to update it every time you recalculate your carbon footprint or make an important change to, or progress in, your emissions reduction strategy. But mostly, it's there to tell the story of what sustainability means to your company.

For publicly traded companies, brand-level marketing might also include press releases. Most often, these will be focused on major sustainability accomplishments or goal-setting. If your company became carbon neutral in the year prior or joined a major climate action group in your industry, or set a net-zero target, you will want to share those in press releases and update your sustainability page when the time is right.

The brand marketing level is where all of your social media promotions, especially the very popular Earth Day or Earth Month content, will live. When your marketing team comes up with campaigns tied to national movements around climate, you're building your brand as a sustainable company.

The last part of sustainable brand building is industry leadership. Once you feel that you have taken enough real action in sustainability to speak credibly on the topic, start by putting your executives on sustainability panels and speaker tracks at industry conferences. Use those opportunities to educate and inspire the customers you have in attendance. Don't focus on patting yourself on the back or sharing how your sustainability efforts are going to save the world. Focus your communication on education, humility, transparency, and action.

Sustainability, unlike almost any other part of corporate strategy, is made more successful if your competitors are as good as you are. If your company reduces emissions and does sustainability well, but your competitors do not, the world is still in a very bad place. We want all companies to measure and reduce emissions, and sustainability shouldn't be a trade secret. It doesn't help your stakeholders if you figure out sustainability but others in your industry don't know where to start. Teaching others exactly what your company is doing to measure and reduce your emissions and openly sharing your challenges and accomplishments will earn you the credibility you're looking for as a sustainable brand.

Technology company Atlassian embraced this concept and published a guide for the technology industry to decarbonize their operations. Cleverly titled *Don't $!@# The Planet*, Atlassian wants to empower every single technology company, including all of its competitors, to do sustainability as well as it does. This type of brand-level marketing effort cements Atlassian's standing as a company that takes sustainability seriously, and the tens of thousands of media hits that its climate-focused PDF guide received helped the sustainability team request further investment.

You can do something similar for your industry and improve your standing as a brand that truly cares about sustainability by teaching others in your industry – even competitors – how to take action around climate change.

## Action-triggered marketing

In action-triggered sustainability marketing, you're engaging with your customers on a more personal, transactional level. Every time a customer purchases your product, you have an opportunity to bring sustainability into the interaction. Companies can use that moment to offer information or to engage the customer further in the sustainability journey.

For example, every time you place an online food order with Chipotle, the receipt you receive in your email contains sustainability information. It will tell you things like how much carbon and water were used in creating your meal. Chipotle did work to customize the findings to each customer's specific order, a powerful touch of transparency in sustainability marketing.

Other restaurants do this more passively by carbon-labeling their menus. Just Salad, a New York-based salad chain, calculated the emissions associated with every meal on its menu and listed the data right next to the calorie count. In this way, it engages customers right at the point of purchase and makes sustainability part of its customers' table talk.

Other companies choose to engage their customers more directly in the sustainability journey. Tiny Earth Toys, a subscription children's toy company, includes a slip of paper with every toy delivery that teaches parents how to return the toys when children grow out of them. It explains how its circular toy program works and encourages parents to take good care of the toys so they can be reused by other children.

Many other companies, especially those with their own carbon neutrality commitments, invite customers to purchase carbon offsets at checkout. Rental car companies like Enterprise, airlines like United, e-commerce brands like Etsy, and restaurants like Elephante in Los Angeles all ask their customers at checkout to add a small amount to the bill to move capital into climate action. These companies are putting something on the line to move sustainability forward. It's always hard to ask your customer for more money right before checkout; it risks turning the customer away and losing the entire sale. But by doing this, these companies engage their customers in a climate conversation at every interaction and move a significant amount of capital to combat climate change.

Even B2B software companies can integrate action-triggered sustainability into their customer interactions. Stripe, the software company that enables payments across much of the internet, has a product called Stripe Climate. The businesses that use Stripe for payments can enable Stripe Climate on their checkout page and automatically move a predetermined, small percentage of revenue into important climate initiatives. This sort of interaction helps make Stripe seem like a climate leader to its customers while also helping its millions of customers enable action-triggered sustainability marketing of their own.

Customer-directed sustainability marketing is as complex and nuanced as all other types of marketing. You'll want to be thoughtful in your approach, thinking strategically from the brand level and digging deep to implement climate into every customer interaction. And make sure you measure the results of your work by tracking everything that marketing usually tracks – impressions, conversions, and attribution. Sustainability teams who can find ROI in their climate marketing are going to be more successful in building and expanding their programs.

Communicating to employees is often voluntary marketing, and marketing to customers can be either required reporting or voluntary. But communication to the last important stakeholder – the investor – is driven almost exclusively by reporting requirements.

## INVESTORS

As described in the introduction, investors comprise one of the strongest forces pushing corporate sustainability forward. As

Deloitte, the global consulting firm, says on the page promoting its ESG-advisory business:

> *"In a survey of senior executives, 97 percent said that external stakeholders have the most influence on a company's ESG reporting and disclosure policy. These stakeholders understand this work is much bigger than a simple tick-the-box exercise. Because it's about business fundamentals. It's about risk and opportunity. It's about strategy and company performance and unlocking future value. And investors want to know how you're taking action."*

It finishes with research from its 2022 *Ingraining Sustainability in the Next Era of ESG Investing* study, saying that "54 percent of managed investment assets will be ESG-mandated by 2024."

It is literally good business to have a well-run sustainability program. Investors believe that companies that are prepared to comply with global regulations and that appreciate the importance of sustainability to employees and customers will be more successful in the long term. But that is only true if an investor considering your company can learn about the work you are doing.

Most companies will have both inbound and outbound communication requests from investors. Often, you won't need to address investor communication until you've started to receive inbound requests. Companies might get to this stage as they raise money from late-stage capital ("Series D" in venture capital terms) or ESG-focused funds. Only larger companies will ever need to create investor-focused ESG reports. This may become relevant if your company is preparing for an IPO or is already publicly traded.

Let's start with requests. Most inbound investor requests will be fairly simple. At the very least, they will ask you for your carbon footprint. While some might want to know your Scope 1–3 emissions, the majority will be content with your Scope 1 and 2 emissions. They are looking for this sort of data so they can tell their limited partners, who have their own sustainability requirements, that they have met certain sustainability targets and have made at least some progress in measuring and reducing the emissions of their portfolio.

More advanced investors may ask about carbon-neutral commitments and timelines. These investors are likely to provide some sort of support to meet these goals. Some might go so far as to fund a portion of the carbon neutrality effort, or provide their own ESG resources to make this work easier for their portfolio companies.

A good example of this is HG Capital, a large software and healthcare private equity investor. It's been leading on the sustainability front for years and already has sophisticated carbon footprint reports of its own. The company is itself carbon neutral and reports publicly on carbon emissions and carbon intensity per employee and per billion dollars under management. In addition to setting its own science-based targets (SBT, a climate framework we'll explore later in this chapter) of 50 percent emissions reduction by 2030, the firm set public targets for its portfolio companies:

- 26 percent of our invested capital will be covered by SBTs by 2026
- 50 percent of our invested capital will be covered by SBTs by 2030
- 100 percent of our invested capital will be covered by SBTs by 2040

To measure and achieve these goals, HG Capital surveys its portfolio companies annually on their progress. It provides support in the form of negotiated partnerships with approved carbon-accounting software, an ESG team to support any portfolio company, and conferences for the executives from their portfolio companies to share best practices and learnings from ESG work.

Regardless of how much help you get from an investor, it will fall to you – the person leading sustainability – to answer inbound requests. You will need to have this data at your fingertips so you and your colleagues can easily report to your investors.

You will also want to make it easy for your CEO and CFO to access the latest sustainability data whenever they need it. If sustainability requests are starting to come in, your board of directors will likely ask your executives to report on progress often. You will have an advantage if you make it easy for the executives who present to your board to look up your carbon footprint data and, ideally, some great charts showing progress, whenever they need to. Help them look good to investors and the board by putting this data at their fingertips, and they will give you the resources you need to continue to make the company's emissions charts go down and to the right.

More sophisticated sustainability programs will publish ESG reports (also named "impact reports" or "sustainability reports".) These reports can range in length from a one-page factsheet to a hundred-page novella (Apple's 2022 *Environmental Report* is 128 pages) and can cover everything from community services and volunteer efforts to carbon footprint data and new plastic-free product lines.

These reports are investor-focused. Your primary goal is not to inspire employees or excite customers, although these might be nice ancillary effects. It is to tell the investment markets that your company appreciates the requirements and responsibilities of a modern company to make progress on environmental issues. Investors reading the report want to see that you are doing the right things, have an appropriate degree of transparency, and are making progress. They want to have the conviction that your company has a role to play in the new green economy. If they believe you, they'll use it as part of their reasoning to support a "buy" or "hold" position. If they don't see you fitting into a sustainable future, they'll wonder what else your company is missing.

In your sustainability report (or at least the sustainability section of your ESG report), you will want to pack a lot of relevant sustainability information into just a few pages. You'll want to share your carbon footprint for the past year, highlight improvements, and acknowledge opportunities for growth. You should explain your carbon neutrality or net-zero strategy if you have those and be clear about how you are expecting to improve.

As always, you want to focus on action and transparency. Talk about the programs you are implementing to reduce emissions for yourself and your customers. For example, the payments technology company Zuora describes how its payments software enables customers to create subscription business models that reduce waste and increase the adoption of electric vehicle charging. HR software company Zendesk links to its *Supplier Code of Conduct* and the new sustainability clause its team put in it. YUM! Brands (owners of Taco Bell, Pizza Hut, and KFC) publishes every single one of its planet-related goals and documents its progress, whether it is on pace or behind.

And share specifics around your carbon footprint and your progress. Transparency builds trust. Even if your carbon emissions increased year over year because of acquisitions or growth in the business, don't shy away from an honest review of the data. If the data shows emissions are going up, don't try to hide behind complexity. Show the data exactly as it appears, then go take action to make your numbers better for next year.

Whether you do it voluntarily or because of customer or investor demand, you may be required to take your reporting further. This involves aligning to a sustainability framework.

## CLIMATE FRAMEWORKS

All sustainability frameworks have the same goal: standardizing the reporting of a complicated topic to give stakeholders a common language to judge progress. However, there is an alphabet soup of sustainability frameworks your company could comply with: GRI, SASB, TCFD, IR, SDG, DJSI. It can be difficult to decide what to do, which to start with, or even whether to take up this path at all.

It helps to know that each framework comes at the issues from different angles. Some are focused on certain industries (Task-Force on Climate-Related Financial Disclosures is built for the financial sector) while others are inclusive of a suite of issues (the United Nations Sustainable Development Goals cover everything from water use to women's education).

Setting targets and reporting into frameworks helps companies build a long-term mindset of sustainability. Setting a goal on its own does not reduce emissions. But communicating to the world that your sustainability work is important, that you're willing to put your name on the line for it, and that you've done the hard work required to report into these frameworks, shows all of your stakeholders that the fight against climate change is an issue your company is fully behind.

These frameworks also create durability and a continuity that other commitments might lack. If you have a CEO who is currently excited about sustainability and builds out a department to work on strategy, there is no guarantee that the next CEO won't decide to disband all sustainability efforts, seeing them as a distraction and a waste of time.

It's the corporate version of a presidential executive order versus a bill passed through Congress. Executive orders are great, but new presidents can wipe them out as easily as they can instill new ones. Bills turned into law by Congress, however, hold steady through any presidential hand off.

Publicly communicated commitments, done through internationally recognized frameworks, hold your company accountable for the duration of that goal, just as a bill signed into law by Congress holds the country permanently accountable. Of course, the next CEO can do whatever they want and might still believe sustainability efforts to be a poor use of time, but they will be very hesitant to cut funding and support for a solid, public commitment the company has already made.

We're going to focus on just three frameworks: CDP, SBTi, and Net Zero, as these are the most likely to pertain to a company early in its sustainability journey.

## CDP

The Carbon Disclosure Project (CDP) is a global environmental disclosure platform that provides companies with a comprehensive framework to assess and manage their impact on the environment. CDP enables companies to report on their carbon emissions and other environmental impacts, and provides a platform for investors to access environmental data from companies they invest in.

Over 15,000 companies from almost every industry have submitted to CDP. Questions range from asking about your carbon footprint to learning how well your company understands climate risk, and the letter grade you earn relates more to the data and defensibility of your answers than how low your emissions are.

A company's first interaction with CDP often comes from a customer request. Both large companies and the federal government are moving towards CDP as the single source of truth in supply-chain climate data. Smaller companies can often put off the CDP process as burdensome for a few years and focus on reporting emissions. But this framework is growing rapidly, so anyone with customers in the Fortune 1000 is likely to come across CDP in the next few years.

The process of applying to CDP involves the following steps:

1. Register: Companies must first register with CDP and provide details about their operations and emissions.

2. Complete the disclosure questionnaire: Companies must then complete a comprehensive questionnaire that covers their emissions, energy use, water use, deforestation, and other environmental impacts. The questionnaire typically launches in April and closes in August. Completing it can take several weeks.

3. Verify data: Companies must then verify their data to ensure its accuracy and reliability.

4. Report: Companies must then report their data to CDP and make it publicly available.

## SBTi

Science-based targets (SBT) is an initiative that helps companies set and achieve science-based emissions reduction targets. SBT aims to align companies' emissions reduction efforts with the latest scientific understanding of what is necessary to limit global warming to well below 2°C and pursue efforts to limit it to 1.5°C, as specified in the Paris Agreement. Companies that adopt SBT set targets based on rigorous science covering their entire value chain. The targets cover the most significant greenhouse gas emissions, including direct and indirect emissions.

Science-based targets are difficult to meet and shouldn't be set lightly. It requires buy-in from your full executive team and your board, as you'll be setting commitments that are likely to outlast any of your current leaders. This makes sense, as climate change happens on a time horizon that companies are not used to operating under. But it will be difficult for your executive team to make a commitment so far out unless they deeply understand the benefits and what's required.

When the technology company New Relic took this path, it took almost a year of preparation, pre-work, and executive education before any science-based target could be set. As sustainability director Simone Wren said in an April 2023 interview:

"A key piece of our work started this time last year. We did the work last year to measure our GHG emissions. We took that information and made sure we were crafting a strategy that is in accordance with that data.

It starts, as many ESG journeys do, with a materiality study to understand which pieces are material to our various stakeholders. Then gathering the data for our emissions footprint was the next step. We then engaged a consulting firm to help build out our climate strategy. They looked at our footprint data. We talked to the individual owners of the pieces of the business that drive those emissions and started talking to them about what a more emissions-aware approach to their work might be. That was a many months-long process of conversation and taking guesses at what might work for our business and validating those guesses. As with anything, we had to make sure it was approved by our leadership and by our board. And then writing a press release and getting it out into the world.

As important as setting those targets and being very careful about how to arrive at those targets is, what's really important is the work that's ahead of us. How to reduce our emissions and building it into the way our business functions."

As the company learned more about the role SBTs play in corporate sustainability, it found the courage to set its own targets. In March 2023 it announced, "New Relic believes that by adhering to science-backed emissions targets, the business will be well-positioned for long-term growth and competitive differentiation in the market, while doing its part to slow climate change and pave the path toward decarbonization."

The process of applying to SBT involves the following steps:

1. Conduct a greenhouse gas (GHG) emissions inventory: Companies must first conduct an assessment of their GHG emissions to determine the scope of their impact on the environment.

2. Set targets: Based on their GHG emissions inventory, companies must then set science-based targets that align with the Paris Agreement. The targets must be ambitious, stretching, and achievable, and must cover their entire value chain.

3. Seek validation: Companies must then seek validation from SBT for their targets to ensure they are science-based and align with the Paris Agreement.

4. Implementation: Once the targets are validated, companies must implement them and regularly report on their progress towards achieving them.

## NET ZERO

Net Zero is a subset of Science Based Targets that includes verified carbon removal. This is the most ambitious corporate sustainability commitment, locking companies in for decades of hard work, relying on yet-unthought-of technological advances to decarbonize. Like carbon neutrality, which will be discussed in more detail in the next chapter, Net Zero Science Based Targets requires a plan to reach zero emissions by a certain date.

To do this, you follow many of the same steps as you would when setting a science-based reduction target. Work hard to reduce the absolute emissions, not emissions intensity, across whatever Scopes you commit to. Once you've reduced everything you're able to, your company needs to purchase verified carbon removal or offsets to reach the "net zero" standard.

As the Science Based Targets initiative writes:

*"A company is only considered to have reached net-zero when it has achieved its long-term science-based target. Most companies are required to have long-term targets with emission reductions of at least 90 percent by 2050. At that point, a company must use carbon removals to neutralize any limited emissions that cannot yet be eliminated."*

In other words, it takes serious commitment over many years to reach a net-zero goal. These goals should not be set lightly. It's hard to reach net zero. There are not currently any fines or massive penalties for missing goals, but there will be social consequences and bad press if your company isn't moving in that direction.

Communication is one of the most challenging and nuanced aspects of sustainability. We've seen how required reporting, as requested by customers and investors, and voluntary marketing are opportunities to build employee and customer engagement. They require thoughtful work based on action and transparency.

The most ambitious of your communication efforts will often include carbon offsets – a controversial topic we'll cover in the next chapter.

## SUMMARY

- Required reporting involves sharing carbon footprint data with customers and investors and reporting to climate frameworks.
- Voluntary marketing can be an opportunity to build a strong brand that excites employees and customers.
- Any sustainability communication should be based on action and transparency.

## ACTIONS

While your plans will depend on your industry, regulatory environment, and customer base, there remain a few set rules on how to communicate about sustainability. Below is the process I would follow for almost any company starting its sustainability program from scratch (table 5.1).

**Table 5.1.** How to build a successful sustainability communication strategy

| Organize | Organize all existing sustainability programs into one document. |
|---|---|
| Engage employees | Make your initial communications internal. Start by building channels among non-management employees to test if this matters to your peers. |
| Engage leadership | Make sustainability a topic among executive and board-level leadership. |
| Set goals | Set sustainability goals internally. Get alignment and approval from executives. |
| Make tangible progress on goals | This isn't exclusively the marketing team's job, but no marketing should happen until you have tangible progress to talk about. |
| Build page without fanfare | Launch an external-facing sustainability page that is transparent about where you are at today, what you are working on, and what you hope to accomplish. |
| Test customer marketing | Run small tests promoting sustainability to customers. Limited email campaigns, social media posts, or blogs. Avoid grand statements or overly ambitious commitments. Measure response. |
| Set targets | Set a carbon neutrality goal or submit to frameworks like CDP or SBTi. |
| Build industry leadership | Move your industry towards sustainability by speaking at conferences, releasing guidance based on your own progress, and openly sharing challenges. |
| Increase sustainability in traditional marketing | Over time, increase the scope of your communications. Always focus on action and transparency. |

You will need to adapt your actual work to what you know about your industry, company, customers, and investors. But if you follow the above path, and consistently focus on action and transparency, you'll be able to build a successful sustainability communication strategy with real ROI for your teams.

*Chapter 6*

## CARBON OFFSETS

Carbon offsets are the gateway drug to sustainability. They are one of the first things you learn about as you begin to explore the corporate sustainability movement. And just as drug users discover with their narcotic counterpart, you quickly learn two important things. First, carbon offsets definitely get you high (or, at least, excited to explore other aspects of sustainability). And second, offsetting is not enough on its own.

Carbon offsets are the most capitalistic response to the negative effects of capitalism on the environment. It's as if someone said, "Let's create a market, driven by the laws of supply and demand, that allows companies to pay a fee and make sustainability problems go away." Indeed, the 2018 Nobel Prize for Economics went to Yale professor Bill Nordhaus, who spent his career writing about carbon taxes, carbon pricing, and cap and trade systems. Carbon offsets are an economist's solution to an environmentalist's issue.

While carbon offsets have many issues (it's common to see articles about a wasteful offset project or a greenwashing accusation tied to low-quality offsets), they are acknowledged to be a key part of the fight against climate change. Consulting firms have done studies, corporations have invested millions, and climate organizations have determined their value. Carbon offsets matter, and they're important to understand.

So how do you navigate this moral and practical maze? In this chapter, we'll explore the history of carbon offsets, different types of offset projects, how to think about offsets and carbon neutrality in your corporate sustainability strategy, and how to communicate about your offset purchases. We'll begin with the basics of how they work.

## HOW CARBON OFFSETS WORK

Carbon offsets allow an individual or company to balance out their carbon emissions (all the things they do that harm the environment) by investing in projects around the world that remove carbon or avoid the emission of additional carbon. Each ton of carbon removed or avoided is called one carbon offset, or carbon credit. If you purchase carbon offsets equivalent to the total amount of carbon your company emits in a year, you can claim carbon neutrality.

Used well, carbon neutrality is a useful tool that puts a sort of tax on companies. It incentivizes them to reduce their emissions so they can spend less money on carbon offsets. And it funds the development of environmentally important projects through an economically liquid market. Carbon offsets, at their best, are what consulting firm McKinsey (a high-volume buyer of offsets) calls a "crucial part of the effort to achieve net-zero emissions."

But at its worst, carbon neutrality is a cheap marketing trick, providing what the *Financial Times* called "a license to pollute." For example, if your company measured its carbon footprint to be 1,000 mt of CO2e (the footprint of an average restaurant) and purchased carbon offsets at a very cheap $3/ton (just a few clicks and a credit card payment on many websites!), you could brag to the world about being a carbon-neutral business that cares about the climate. All for the cost of $3,000, or two days' revenue at a typical New York City sandwich shop. Then, you can go even further and invest $20,000 in an advertising campaign about your business's responsibility to the planet and doing the right thing because you care.

In other words, a business can make a small financial investment in projects of debatable environmental value, make zero effort to reduce emissions, and still brand itself as sustainable. Emissions go up the following year? Just buy a few more carbon offsets; a free license to pollute.

This carbon-neutral world is a status quo nirvana in which the planet and economic growth can coexist. How lovely. Unfortunately, the answers are never quite as simple as we'd like them to be. How frustrating that must be for all the CEOs and marketing executives hoping to take advantage of their sudden passion for the planet!

The carbon offset market then, like any complicated, ambitious, and relatively young industry, has flaws. As with any product, "cheap" and "good" are often contradictory. If you want quality, you need to pay for it. If you want cheap, you're going to sacrifice quality. High-quality carbon offsets are expensive because they take significant capital to execute, validate, and maintain. At their best, carbon offsets can be an important weapon against climate change. When they are high quality, they remove measurable and significant amounts of $CO_2$ (or avoid adding more $CO_2$) from the air to counteract human pollution. But when they are cheap, they're little more than a way for companies to write a check and absolve their sins.

The three most important flaws in the eternal search for cheap but good offsets are:

1. Temporary time frame of carbon sequestration (also called permanence)
2. An offset might simply move emissions from one place to another (also called leakage)

3. Purchasing an offset doesn't necessarily do anything new for the planet (also called additionality)

Cheap offsets often lack permanence. One of the most common offset project types is forest preservation. The idea is that if a company purchases carbon offsets to protect a forest, then the owners of that forest won't chop it down and sell the trees to a mill and the land to a developer. When it works as it's supposed to, it's definitely a good thing to have more trees. But sadly, it's never that easy in practice. Trees, while important for the climate, do not sequester carbon permanently. Over the course of a tree's 100-year-long life, a tree might absorb one ton of carbon. Multiply by millions of trees in a large forest, and that's a big deal.

But once that tree dies due to age, disease, natural fires, human logging, or (most ironically) climate change-induced problems, carbon is once more released into the atmosphere. Protecting a forest is, in theory, pretty cheap. It's already there, so let's give someone money to not chop it down. But a small amount of money can't keep trees alive forever, so carbon will eventually be released into the atmosphere. No permanence.

Cheap offsets also often suffer from leakage. Leakage is an offshoot of economics' most classic maxim – supply and demand. If people need to use, or are able to sell, a resource, they'll find a way to get it. If one part of a forest is protected from being cut down by carbon offsets, then loggers might easily go to another part of the forest. If a carbon offset market is created to fund the destruction of a specific type of refrigerant, some enterprising capitalist might start to manufacture that very refrigerant to get paid for its destruction. Leakage is difficult to measure and needs good policy to be controlled.

Cheap offsets, especially when applied to nature-based solutions, also lack additionality. Additionality means that the money put towards the offset created a carbon removal or avoidance that would never have happened without that investment. With technology-based offsets like direct air capture, additionality is pretty obvious. There is no business opportunity for a giant vacuum cleaner that sucks carbon out of the air without the carbon offset market. Without the $10,000 given by a company looking to mediate its carbon emissions, a direct air capture plant could never run. That money helps generate a carbon offset that is additional.

While additionality is often clear in technical solutions (if there is no market for a new product, only offsets can fund its development), it can be harder to ascribe additionality to nature-based solutions like forest preservation. If a forest has been standing for 1,000 years, will your money really keep it standing for an additional year?

In one egregious example that illustrates the point, a billionaire landowner in New Jersey decided to turn his 3,800-acre hunting ground into a carbon offset project. He brought in a verifier, put a price on the carbon his forest removes each year, and started selling over three million credits. Some well-meaning company somewhere, hoping to do something good for the world, purchased these offsets, likely at a pretty low price, because it was 100 percent profit margin for the landowner. The company made a carbon neutrality statement, told its employees and customers, and was rightfully proud of itself.

But it turns out that all the money spent on carbon offsets generated from that forest was neither permanent nor additional. The landowner could change his mind next year, cut down all the trees, make a killing on timber sales, and all the sequestered $CO_2$ would be back in the atmosphere. A wildfire could burn up a portion of the forest, releasing $CO_2$ back into the atmosphere. Permanence, as defined on a scale of 1,000 years, is just impossible with trees.

These offsets were obviously not additional. The billionaire landowner never had any intention of clear-cutting the forest he loved to hunt in. He just found another way to make a little more money, and was paid to not do something he never would have done anyway. The offset changed nothing.

If stories of billionaire landowners don't illustrate the point well enough, a romance analogy might help clarify the downside of overreliance on carbon offsets. In 2012, some comedic Brits stood on the streets of London and sold "relationship offsets." The offer seemed amazing. "Do you love cheating on your boyfriend but always feel guilty? We get it! Well, good news, people. Now you can do all the cheating you want, for the low cost of $20! How, you may ask? Well, this new company, Cheat Neutral, will take your $20, keep $5 as a broker fee, and give the remaining $15 to a relationship that remains monogamous. This way, the total amount of monogamy in the world stays the same, and you can keep cheating!" Well, isn't that nice.

This routine would gather just 9,000 views on YouTube; a crime against great political comedy, I think! But their message about the inadequacy of a relationship offset to prevent the consequences of cheating on your spouse carries over brilliantly to the challenge of modern carbon offsets.

When carbon offsets are used poorly, companies think of them as a way of removing all blame and culpability from themselves. Sure, they might have contributed massively to carbon emissions by flying planes, serving steaks, manufacturing plastic bottles, or running their bitcoin mining engines. Sure, they haven't reduced their emissions, nor their emissions intensity, year over year in any significant way. And sure, maybe they polluted a few rivers or clear-cut a few forests.

But c'mon, people! They put their corporate credit card into a website that charged them $5/metric ton of carbon that would be removed by planting trees in Nicaragua! They didn't have to do that.

It was out of the goodness of their heart, and because the CEO truly cares about his grandchildren being able to ski the same Aspen mountains that he and his family have owned… I mean, skied… for generations.

Those are the kind of carbon-offset approaches that make people balk. Those are the offsets mocked by late-night comics like John Oliver, who did an entire feature in August 2022 about the problems with the carbon offset scheme (which now has almost five million views on YouTube). Speaking directly into the camera, Oliver said, "On some level, you probably know that carbon offsets are bullshit, both because you're a reasonably intelligent person and because you know exactly what show you are watching right now. I don't open my beak to squawk out good news."

Those are also the offset strategies that get companies into legal and financial trouble. The advocacy group ClientEarth reports on the many companies that have faced legal action due to poorly representing and falsely advertising the extent of benefits derived from carbon offsets. In its September 2022 briefing on the legal risks of carbon offsets, it said:

*"In the Netherlands, Shell has found itself reprimanded twice in succession, first for advertising '$CO_2$-neutral' car petrol, then for trying a different claim that carbon credits mean '$CO_2$ compensation'. On both occasions, the company was unable to persuade the Dutch advertising watchdog that the offsets advertising was substantiated by the evidence. The airline KLM is facing a court action, supported by ClientEarth, for breaching consumer law with its $CO_2$ compensation marketing. In Germany, a claim is being brought against a list of eight companies, including TotalEnergies, for misleading 'carbon neutral' claims. Legal academics say that using offsets in marketing claims breaches European consumer law standards. The EU Commission has proposed a new 'anti-greenwashing' consumer law, which will place heightened restrictions on 'carbon neutral' claims. In France, after a citizens' assembly called for a ban on 'carbon*

neutral' claims, the legislature enacted a law requiring companies to clarify how emissions are being actually reduced before being offset."

So, that's the argument against carbon offsets. However, when used thoughtfully, carbon offsets provide companies with a very tangible way to make a difference against climate change, spark climate education among employees and customers, and incite real change internally. Well-managed carbon offset projects that can prove higher levels of permanence and additionality, and low leakage, can do genuine good for the world.

The largest companies, many of which boast sustainability teams of dozens of PhDs genuinely dedicated to truth and science, all have carbon offsetting as a core component of their climate strategy. So if Amazon, Google, Uber, and Delta Airlines all have long-term, documented, and well-publicized commitments to carbon offsets, they are not to be ignored. Consulting firm McKinsey even expects the carbon offset market to grow to over $50 billion by 2030.

Carbon offsets are at the center of a modern corporate sustainability strategy. Understanding and advising on how to responsibly leverage them is an important part of a sustainability leader's job. To do this, it helps to understand the intent behind carbon offsets and their relatively short history, which only began just over thirty years ago.

## HISTORY OF THE MARKETS

The first carbon offset program took place in 1989, initiated by an American energy company. Applied Energy Services (AES Corp), founded in 1981, was building momentum and political support behind its plans to manufacture a 183-megawatt coal-fired power plant in Connecticut. In tandem with building this power plant, the company committed $2 million to support the planting of over fifty million trees in the Western Highlands of Guatemala. The company's advisors believed that a financial investment in trees, as non-controversial and hard to argue with as saving puppies or feeding children, would give them the political support needed to build their environmentally plagued coal plant. They were right, and their significant financial contribution over thirty years ago put in place the building of a multi-billion-dollar carbon offset market heralded as everything from climate savior to capitalist fraud.

Over the next decade, many energy companies saw offsets as a viable way of placating critics of the environmental impacts of fossil-fuel-burning plants. Most of the offsets were investments in tree-planting or forestry management schemes. It was the equivalent of the old magician's trick of waving the left hand to distract the audience while the right hand conducts some in-plain-sight mischief. Even today, thirty years later, the carbon markets haven't recovered their reputation of a low-quality veneer that climate polluters use as a cover-up.

But in 1997, with the signing of the Kyoto Protocol, the carbon markets received a major international regulatory boost. The Kyoto Protocol required its 150 signatory countries to put clear limits on carbon emissions. The United States, the world's largest polluter at the time, refused to sign the agreement, so it never acquired the necessary teeth to inspire and enforce real change. Nevertheless, the agreement inspired nations to develop internal carbon emissions measurement and offsetting programs to meet the target climate goals.

This would lead, in 2005, to the world's first and biggest carbon market: The EU Emissions Trading Scheme. The core idea of cap and trade is about rewarding good work and penalizing bad work. The EU, as part of a strong commitment to combat climate change, built a system that would issue a set number of "allowances" to European factories and power plants, permitting emissions up to a certain cap. If your company ended up emitting fewer emissions than your allotted cap, you earned credits that you could sell or "trade." If your business emitted more than your allotted cap, you were required to purchase credits from businesses more successful in reducing their emissions. In this way, good actors (those that reduce emissions) get rewarded and those who aren't able to reduce emissions get fined.

This cap and trade program has helped reduce European emissions in relevant sectors by over 21 percent compared to 2005 levels. But it has a few obvious flaws. First, reducing emissions is difficult. It takes time, capital, and expertise that most companies don't have. If meeting the regulation is as easy as spending a bit of money on someone else's credits, that could be much easier than actually doing the work to reduce emissions.

Similarly, this economic model might create a reverse incentive. If too many companies succeed in lowering emissions and are given credits to sell, the market will be flooded with credits, reducing the fine levied on companies that weren't able to reduce emissions. This happened in 2007 in the EU cap and trade program, when the price of credits went almost to zero.

The European Union cap and trade program was a regional effort, whereas the United Nations' Clean Development Mechanism was a global initiative that came out of the Kyoto Protocol. Today, countries, companies and individuals alike rely on carbon offsets as an important part of a sustainability strategy. For many businesses, beginning with AES back in 1989, it's taken a concerted effort to figure out their role in curbing climate change. And with all this development and iteration, the market for offsets has grown tremendously from about $50 million in annual sales in 2005 to over $2 billion in 2022.

## TYPES OF CARBON OFFSETS

Over the history of the carbon market, dozens of types of carbon offset projects, from forest preservation to high-tech carbon capture, have been developed and sold into the market. When you purchase carbon offsets, you'll often have a wide range of project types and prices to choose from. Let's now look at these various types so we understand what we're buying.

A simple way to divide project types is to differentiate between nature-based carbon offset projects and technology-based projects. Nature-based projects are about protecting the carbon removal that's built into the world already. Most often, these projects involve forests, oceans, and agricultural practices. Technology-based projects use man-made technology to avoid additional emissions and remove carbon. These projects range from cleaning up environmental damage from oil and gas exploration to advanced carbon-removal technologies that take carbon directly out of the air and sequester it underground for thousands of years.

Below is a list of some of the most common carbon offset projects you'll encounter, though it's by no means exhaustive (table 6.1).

## Table 6.1. Categories of carbon offset projects

| Nature / Tech | Type | Description |
| --- | --- | --- |
| Nature | Avoided deforestation | This is the most common carbon offset project type. It involves protecting existing forests from deforestation, degradation, or conversion to other land uses to prevent the release of carbon dioxide that would otherwise be emitted when the trees are cut down. Forest conservation projects typically involve working with local communities and governments to establish protected areas, enforce laws and regulations, and promote sustainable forest management. |
| Nature | Agricultural land management | These carbon offsets support farmers as they adopt new practices and technologies that would reduce greenhouse gas emissions. New farming practices – like no-till farming, cover cropping, and crop rotation – can require significant capital and education. Carbon offsets help fund these changes. |
| Nature | Kelp farming | The ocean, and all the plant life that lives in it, is one of the world's most important carbon sinks. Kelp farming carbon offsets fund the expensive and relatively new efforts to grow kelp, let it absorb carbon, then sink it to the bottom of the ocean where the $CO_2$ can be buried beneath the ocean floor. This is an example of a category of offsets called "blue carbon" that includes similar projects like expanding mangrove forests and restoring salt marshes. |
| Tech | Methane capture | Methane is released from places like landfills and coal mines. Without a carbon offset, owners of those areas have no incentive to invest in the expensive technology needed to capture methane on site. But carbon offsets provide a financial reason to fund the development of on-point methane capture. |
| Tech | Direct Air Capture (DAC) | The best way to imagine DAC is a giant vacuum cleaner that sucks $CO_2$ out of the air and sequesters it in rock and other substances where it is likely to stay for 1,000+ years. While this technology only produces about 4,000 carbon credits annually (about the emissions of three large restaurant locations), it is considered one of the most important technologies for combating climate change. |
| Tech | Refrigerant reclamation | The most commonly used refrigerants today use hydrofluorocarbons, or HFCs. This powerful greenhouse gas is often the highest contributor to emissions for most businesses. Because they are cheap, they are often thrown out after use. Carbon offsets can fund their reclamation and reuse, delaying the release of these noxious gasses. |
| Tech | Improved cookstoves | This popular project combines emissions reduction with important social benefits (often called co-benefits). Many women in developing countries prepare food over open flames using wood or charcoal, both high-emitting energy sources. This offset project funds the development and distribution of clean cookstoves, which use fuel more efficiently and can sometimes run on low-emissions bio fuel. |
| Tech | BECCS (Bioenergy with Carbon Capture and Storage) | BECCS combines biomass energy generation with carbon capture and storage. Biomass, like agricultural residues or energy crops, is used to produce energy, while the carbon dioxide released is captured and stored underground. A biomass power plant burning wood chips captures the emitted $CO_2$ and stores it in suitable geological formations. BECCs provides renewable energy while actively reducing greenhouse gas concentrations. |
| Tech | Biochar | Biochar is produced by heating biomass in a low-oxygen environment. This process, called pyrolysis, causes the biomass to break down into a solid residue (biochar), a liquid (bio-oil), and a gas (bio-gas). Biochar is rich in carbon and can store it for hundreds or thousands of years. It can be deposited in soil where it enriches farmland without producing $CO_2$. |

Each project type scores differently on additionally, permanence and leakage, and offsets can range in price from a few dollars per ton for some afforestation projects to hundreds per ton for newer technological offset projects like direct air capture. Most companies that buy offsets will purchase a portfolio of different projects. A portfolio approach de-risks your use of carbon offsets in case one project loses standing, and allows your company to be involved with high-quality projects in small quantities.

At this point in time, carbon offsets are rarely foolproof. Unless you're spending hundreds of dollars per ton on the highest quality projects, it is difficult to guarantee that your projects won't have some sort of issue. So in the rest of this chapter, we'll discuss what it looks like when offsets are used well and how to communicate about your choice of projects.

## WHEN ARE OFFSETS DONE WELL?

When I started to work in sustainability, I would post about bits of research I'd find, or questions I'd have, or ideas that would come to mind on LinkedIn. My dear Aunt Lyuba, an immigrant from Moscow who continues to admire the incredible comforts provided by capitalism compared to her communist upbringing, balked publicly at one of my posts. "I am for environment protection for sure, but within reason," Lyuba commented. "Can you live without a fridge or AC at this point? I am not. LOL."

Oh, Aunt Lyuba. I'd never ask you to live without your refrigerator. In part because it's important to have some backup frozen foods when we come to your home for dinner, but mostly because the ideal outcome of the sustainability movement is not – and cannot be – a Spartan lifestyle. Yes, we need to reduce the waste that comes from consumerism. But no one wants people to stop buying products and services that make them happy. Yes, businesses should be more thoughtful about unnecessary travel and implement sustainable travel policies. But no executive would want to lose a client because a competitor traveled to visit in person more often than their own climate-conscious sales team. And yes, wouldn't it be nice if we all became vegan and freed cows and chickens to roam newly reforested lands like their wild ancestors? But no, I do not expect the New York City Steakhouse to lose its charm any time soon. Nor will McDonald's fully pivot its $5 billion annual Big Mac business into vegan Impossible Burgers.

Unfortunately for those of us who choose a vegan lifestyle, refuse to fly on planes, or live in a small urban apartment powered by solar energy, most of the world is going to continue to emit $CO_2$. And whatever can't be reduced must be offset.

Carbon offsets are a company's acknowledgement that its main sustainability effort – reducing emissions – still has a ways to go. Carbon offsets are a self-imposed carbon tax. A company that uses carbon offsets declares that "we understand that we create emissions. And we're working on reducing that. But until then, we want to do our part to clean up the world. And if it's going to take us time to reduce our own carbon footprint, perhaps we can support other efforts to remove or avoid additional carbon emissions."

When done well, offsets are a part of the sustainability leader's toolkit. It is not the only solution. It's not even the first. But it is an important contributor to a company's climate strategy. So let's explore how to select projects, how to convince executives that they are worth the money, and how to talk about them to customers, regulators, and employees.

## When Should Offsets Come into Play?

The traditional stance in corporate sustainability is to "reduce everything you can, offset what you can't." Only once your restaurant has built a vegan menu, worked with suppliers to source produce more locally, and bought subway passes for all employees is it time to consider offsets.

Some sustainability leaders take a different approach, however. Right after they measure the company's carbon footprint, they turn immediately to carbon offsets and offset their entire Scope 1–3 footprint. When done immediately like this, offsets serve two purposes.

First, it shows all stakeholders that you are making a very serious financial commitment to taking action on climate. An average restaurant might have emissions of 1,000 mt of $CO_2e$. A software company of 1,000 employees might have emissions of 10,000 mt of $CO_2e$. At $20/ton, that's a cost of $20,000/restaurant or $200,000 for the entire software business. This is a significant budget item that your executives, and likely your board, will need to consider and approve. This harkens to the original use of carbon offsets as a sort of carbon tax, asking companies to pay up in response to their impact on the environment.

That kind of spend gets people's attention. Your marketing team can tell customers that you're a carbon-neutral business. Your recruiting team can tell potential hires that you're the kind of business that takes real action. And, most importantly, you'll have the ear of your executive team, who'll want to know how the company is benefiting from this expense. Using carbon offsets lets a company take real action on climate change that it can be proud of.

And as we'll discuss further in Chapter 7, this is the right way to build executive support for your sustainability work; give your executives what they want. Show your leadership that the way to help them succeed in their jobs is to give you the resources to succeed in yours. Tie the company's success to your success.

While carbon-neutral claims have their flaws, they provide a very clear, immediate win that you can deliver for your entire team.

You need to be honest with yourself, your peers, and your external stakeholders that carbon neutrality isn't the final goal; it's the first step. But it's a first step that can drive real progress.

The second benefit is that your carbon-offset spend becomes a sort of bargaining chip as you begin to ask for a budget towards initiatives that will lower your carbon footprint. If you haven't yet spent any money on sustainability and ask your executives for $10,000 to install cleaner kitchen grills, they will look at that expense as a brand-new line item. If, however, you're able to show them that this $10,000 expense will reduce your emissions by 100 mt of $CO_2e$ per year, lowering your carbon offset expenditure by $2,000 per year, you've now built a very clear payback period and business case.

Jared Ingersoll, former head of sustainability at Canva, told me that he called this strategy a "leverage against risk." When Jared took over, Canva had already made a commitment to be carbon neutral, so it knew it was going to purchase carbon offsets. Pulling out of that commitment would be a market risk.

Jared knew that offsets would become more expensive in future. So he built a chart estimating what the cost of carbon neutrality would be in ten years' time if the price of both carbon offsets and the company's carbon emissions continued to increase. The chart visibly demonstrated the rapidly increasing cost of maintaining carbon neutrality and scared the CFO into asking, "How do we avoid the risk of this cost?"

That one question gave Jared the leverage to ask for investments that would reduce emissions. An expense today that reduces emissions and avoids the increasing cost of offsets forevermore was worth a ton to the company. There was genuine financial risk in not reducing emissions. Jared took advantage of that and helped Canva build out a world-class emissions reduction program.

## How to pay for carbon offsets

Finding the budget for carbon offsets is a challenge for any business. Whether it's a small independent coffee shop that needs to find $4,000 or a global software company that needs to come up with $400,000, it's a new expense to meet somehow. Here are some leaders explaining where they found the money for carbon offsets and why they decided to prioritize it:

### David Robertson, Owner of Robertson Marketing:

"Our environmental focus is to reduce carbon emissions as much as possible; however, as a small private business, we have budget constraints. Therefore, we rely on a sustainability consultancy to help us identify meaningful carbon offset projects that are high quality yet within our budget. Many of our customers have their own sustainability programs, and they expect us to maintain a formal program as well. Thus, it is important for us to offset our emissions because it illustrates our commitment to environmentally focused business practices which are necessary for existing client relationships and future ones."

### Angus Glover Wilson, Head of Corporate Strategic Operations at Flatiron Health:

"Flatiron Health has been carbon neutral since 2021. For us, this was an executive decision driven by a bunch of factors. A sustainability program takes time to put into place, but this was something we could do immediately. As a software company, our emissions reduction opportunities are limited. Sure, we can commute cleaner or fly less often, but only to an extent. So offsets give us a viable path to make a material impact on sustainability quickly. And the ROI comes from many angles. First, as a mission-driven healthtech company, doing the right thing in all aspects of life is especially important to us as a business and individually. People with cancer are one population that stands to suffer disproportionately from the impacts of climate change, so it's consistent with our mission to look to mitigate those impacts. Second, as a transparent organization that genuinely cares for the well-being of its employees, we want to help them feel coherence between how they live outside of work, and how they show up at work. Creating the conditions for us to be at least as environmentally responsible in the work context as at home (if not more so) is a key part of that, which speaks both to current employees and to folks considering joining us. And third, our customers are also mission-driven, and with their own sustainability imperatives. Carbon offsets allow us to demonstrate a material commitment even as we incubate our less-visible direct reduction efforts."

If your company doesn't have the money to spend on carbon offsets out of an existing budget, you can involve your customers to help. Elephante, a Los Angeles restaurant and part of the Wish You Were Here group, did this by adding a standard 0.5 percent fee to every customer bill and moving all of that money into carbon offset purchases. It added a QR code to its menu linking to a website on carbon neutrality, explaining the types of carbon offsets the restaurant supports and encouraging customers to learn how it works. It also lets any customer opt out by checking a box on their receipt. In this way, a local restaurant sourced the money for carbon neutrality from customers while inserting sustainability as a talking point at the table. The company committed to filling any gap in funds needed to reach carbon neutrality, but customer involvement got them most of the way there.

Enterprise Rent-A-Car started a similar program back in 2008. Customers who rent a car through Enterprise are asked to give $1.25, which will go towards purchasing carbon offsets. The program has been successful. In its very first year of operation, over 175,000 customers opted to contribute $1.25 to carbon offsets, and every dollar was matched by the company. This led to $440,000 being moved to carbon offsets in just twelve months. However, the challenge for Enterprise is communication. If I rent a gas-guzzling Ford Mustang (the original, not the cool new electric one) for five days and 500 miles of California driving, it's ludicrous to assume that $1.25 will offset the entirety of my trip. Enterprise even got into some trouble for greenwashing as it was mentioned in the 2022 John Oliver clip on the topic of carbon offsets.

What it should have done instead was focus on transparency. The company needed to explain to customers that Enterprise uses carbon offsets as a small part of its sustainability strategy. While $1.25 won't offset all the emissions of a trip, it will contribute to positive change that wouldn't have happened otherwise. Enterprise could have used this opportunity to educate customers about what a carbon offset is. It could have leaned into transparency and talked about what percentage of the money goes towards purchasing carbon credits (ideally 100 percent), and it could have shown the specific projects it was supporting. It could have also used this moment to show a commitment to action. Talking about the company's move to an electric or hybrid fleet would have put carbon offsets into context as just one part of a corporate sustainability strategy instead of the whole thing.

Once you decide that carbon offsets should be a part of your sustainability strategy and you've decided on a budget, you'll need to go ahead and make the purchase. Unfortunately, you don't just go to the carbon offset store and buy a few tons of carbon offsets off the shelf. So let's look at your options when it comes to sourcing.

## A BUYER'S GUIDE TO CARBON OFFSETS

In 2023, I was helping a publicly traded technology company purchase about 20,000 carbon credits. The Chief Legal Counsel asked me for a few examples of the kinds of carbon offset projects available so she could consider which category of offset made the most sense for the company's brand story and values.

I reached out to multiple brokers and offset developers and provided a few specifications. The client was looking for about 20,000 credits at $15–20/ton and preferred the projects aligned with the company's existing values and priorities of supporting investments in diversity, technology, or education. It took a few emails back and forth with the brokers as I narrowed in on three projects that I thought were most relevant: all, coincidentally, verified by the American Carbon Registry. On the next call with the Chief Legal Counsel, I presented the projects and shared what I liked about them.

She asked, "So interesting. How did you source these? Did you just visit the website of the American Carbon Registry and pick these out?"

"Unfortunately not," I told her. "These transactions are still very manual. Imagine buying stocks in the 1980s. Pink slips, phone calls, negotiations. That's much closer to it than the way we buy anything else today."

The way carbon offset projects are bought and sold today are, for the most part, highly inefficient. A project developer takes responsibility for bringing the project to life. They fund the work it takes to run the biochar facility or protect the forest or run a refrigerator reclamation project.

They then work with a verifier to measure the validity of their carbon offset claims. For the most part, the verification process is managed by three large international organizations: Verra, The American Carbon Registry, and The Gold Standard. One of these groups is contracted to come in and provide some scientific guidance around the number of carbon credits the project can claim in one year.

Next, the project developer needs to find buyers for its credits. To do this, they often contract with a collection of brokers who work to connect buyer and seller. These brokers might win the loyalty of the project developer by pre-buying credits or guaranteeing a certain amount of sales. The offset broker, just like the 1980s stockbroker of old, will then make it their job to try and sell carbon offsets to whomever they can find to buy them.

At times, the brokers might sell directly to a company that will retire, or claim, the credit. Other times, there might be a few more stages before the credit is finally retired. Consultants or carbon accounting firms might want to add carbon offsets to their product mix to sell them directly to their own customers and streamline the whole experience.

Each of these parties – project developers, verifiers, brokers, and final points of sale – need to take a certain amount of margin on the sale of the offset. So if a final buyer pays $20 for a carbon credit, it's very possible that only $5–10 of that money actually goes to the project developer who did the hard work of removing carbon from the atmosphere.

This is, of course, a problem for anyone who cares about seeing their dollar make an impact. It may be disheartening to a company to learn that if they commit $100,000 to the purchase of carbon offsets, believing it to be an important step in their climate strategy, $50,000 of those dollars are taken by middlemen.

A modern, tech-savvy reader might think the solution is obvious! Build a marketplace where project creators can list their projects directly, cutting out the middlemen. Basically, build E-Trade, but for carbon offsets. It's a great idea, and you wouldn't be the first to have it. Multiple technology companies are competing to become the marketplace of choice for carbon offsets, streamlining the buying process, lowering the price of offsets, and moving more money towards the environmental effort they're meant to support. A quick Google search for "carbon offset marketplace" will lead you to a dozen options working on this problem.

So there are multiple ways to purchase offsets – through your carbon accounting software or consultant, through a broker, through a marketplace, or directly through the carbon offset project developer. Which of these makes the most sense?

We can disregard the direct purchase almost immediately. While that model cuts out middlemen and moves the most money to climate efforts, it's only available to companies buying massive quantities of carbon offsets, likely millions of tons. Project developers don't want to work with multiple purchasers – that's why they work with brokers. They're focused on making the offset work well, not selling the offset.

Buying offsets through whatever partner is supporting your sustainability work so far, typically a carbon accounting software company or consultant, is the easiest option. If you're working with people you like and trust, you can continue to deepen and support that relationship. Your procurement and legal teams will be happy too. You won't need to go through additional vetting of new companies, security measures, or any other of the usual processes when you have a new supplier.

If they're any good, your sustainability partner will work hard to give you a variety of offset options, as they can buy from across multiple brokers and marketplaces and maximize for variety. Many of these groups also buy offsets in bulk to help lower the cost for you. If you need to purchase 1,000 carbon credits, a broker or marketplace might get you a price of $20/ton at a total cost of $20,000. But your carbon accounting partner might have agreements to pre-buy 50,000 tons at a cost of $15/ton, passing along some of those savings to you.

You can also reach out to brokers directly. A Google search for "carbon offset broker" will show you many companies. Verification companies sometimes sell the offsets they verify (with a slight conflict of interest!). And newer technology companies have been competing to become more modern brokers.

Your money will be a little closer to the end project but because of smaller buying power and a new relationship, you may end up paying a higher price per ton. Though, as a savvy buyer, you can do the work to compare prices across brokers and negotiate against the initial offer. Multiple brokers might even have access to the same carbon offset projects, so you'll be able to see directly how different brokers price things.

You will, however, need to go through the pains and internal challenges of onboarding a new partner. Your legal and procurement teams are likely to get involved in reviewing contracts, approving suppliers, and getting all of that set up. Depending on the quantity of offsets you're buying, this may be worth it. But for many companies, it could just be an additional burden.

Your last option is to go through a marketplace, a modern technology company like Pachama, Patch.io or Flowcarbon. These companies are attempting to do for offsets what E-Trade did for stocks in the 1990s; use technology to add a layer of transparency above an otherwise manual system. For the most part, their idea is the right one and is just *so* Silicon Valley. Remove the friction from purchasing a simple asset! Put carbon offsets on the blockchain! Bring efficiency to an inefficient market!

Marketplaces *are* the right answer. They should exist, will exist, and will lower the cost of carbon offsets while increasing the amount of capital that goes directly to a project. But like all new technologies, it will take some time for these marketplaces to develop the secure backend that it took brokers decades to build.

Marketplaces also have the theoretical advantage of variety. They have the opportunity for scale across many projects and brokers. But you're going to lose your ability to negotiate. The list price is what you get, no matter how large your purchase or how many other companies you organize to purchase together.

Additionally, carbon offset marketplaces have only one source of revenue: the margin they make taking your money and getting it to the project developer. To run a healthy tech company, they need to make at least 60 percent margins, which means 60 cents of every dollar you spend on carbon offsets is given to the marketplace. Your sustainability partner, however, already sees you as a profitable customer. You paid for their consulting service or their software, and they want to continue to make you happy and make your sustainability life easier. They are happy to take a smaller margin on any carbon offset purchase. So while the process might be less flexible and choice-filled than with a marketplace, you'll often get more of your money to the final project by working with your sustainability partner and asking them to negotiate on your behalf.

Offsets are a market full of inefficiency. For a company that's proud and excited to spend significant, meaningful capital on a sustainability decision, it's going to be frustrating to realize how little of the money gets to its final destination. But unless you want to do the work of researching projects, finding brokers, negotiating prices, and organizing group purchases, your best bet is still to do what is simplest and most efficient for you. Select the organization you trust and work with already and ask them to help you find the right offsets for your company. Know that this company is likely taking a margin on the sale, and while they deserve to keep a portion of the funds (that's the way they stay in business, of course) you may have some negotiating leverage.

However you buy your carbon offsets, you'll need to be clear on your goals and reasons for doing this work. Many companies aspire to call themselves carbon neutral, proof that they've offset as much $CO_2$ as they've emitted. Carbon neutrality is aspirational for many companies, and imperfect for many others. Go into it with your eyes open, knowing that there are both pros and cons.

## TO BE (CARBON NEUTRAL) OR NOT TO BE (CARBON NEUTRAL)

The core tenet of a good marketing strategy is *simplicity*. Consumers need to feel like they understand what's going on. While people don't want to feel like they're being spoken to like dummies, confusing buyers with nuance is never a winning strategy.

That's why politics can be so polarizing. Nuance is found in the messy middle. It takes time to explain (and even more time to understand) the gray area of any topic. And if a politician ventures into the gray area, they're guaranteed to confuse most of their audience and say something that will upset the remainder.

Carbon neutrality is sustainability's version of avoiding the messy middle. It can be difficult to understand a nuanced offset strategy that a thoughtful, well-informed sustainability team might put together. But do you know what *is* easy to understand? Carbon neutrality. Its definition is right there in the word. When you see that a company is carbon neutral, you don't need to know much about corporate sustainability and carbon accounting to immediately understand that they are neutralizing their impact on the climate. "Must be some pretty nice, caring people there! I'll choose their product over a very similar competitor - why not!"

But as we've seen, carbon neutrality has its flaws. A claim of "carbon neutral" doesn't say anything about the quality of offsets used or the price paid per ton. Two companies with emissions of

1,000 tons $CO_2e$ that want to earn a carbon neutrality claim can take two very different approaches. The first might want high-quality projects at $50/ton, while the second is more budget-conscious and buys the cheapest offsets they can find at $5/ton. Same claim, two very different climate impacts.

And as we've also seen, the news cycle is full of companies getting in trouble for over-promoting a weak carbon neutrality claim. "Carbon neutral" is the right choice for many smaller companies with the budget to buy high-quality offsets that want a simple way to show customers their commitment to sustainability. Larger companies with more to lose in litigation or media hit pieces than they have to gain with a carbon neutrality claim may want to spend their carbon offset budget differently.

I want to suggest an alternative to the easy fix and easily explained Band-Aid of carbon neutrality. It's going to be complicated. Most consumers won't understand it. It'll take up a few paragraphs of your ESG report and won't earn you a pretty badge to put on your packaging.

But it will mean that you are spending money that makes a tangible difference for the planet (gasp!). It will inoculate you from any claims of greenwashing. It will earn you the respect of your industry peers, those with sustainability leaders sick of the oversimplified claims of carbon neutrality and looking for a way to make their company dollars actually work. To quote Mark Trexler, developer of some of the world's first carbon offset projects, "You can maximize for cost-effectiveness or for climate change mitigation. You can't do both." Or as Greg Becker, President and Founder of carbon verification startup Icarus put it more casually, "You can't save the world at five bucks per ton."

So if carbon neutrality isn't a requirement, what other approach can you take? Instead of making claims of carbon neutrality, think and talk about your work as a carbon contribution claim. It's not always about arbitrarily neutralizing the emissions you've measured with offsets of varying prices and qualities. It's about supporting the removal of carbon on a large scale and communicating your contribution to that global effort.

One way to do this is to calculate the cost of becoming fully carbon neutral using lower-cost, verified carbon offset projects. Then instead of buying enough cheap offsets to claim neutrality, move a significant amount of that money to the high end of the market. Spend it on direct air capture at $500/ton. Spend it on biochar at $150/ton.

You will not be able to claim carbon neutrality. You won't be able to say you fully offset the emissions from any significant part of your business. You won't get a pretty little badge on your website. Badges to commend valuable carbon contribution claims don't yet exist in as simple a format as carbon neutrality badges, though perhaps they should. Yet while expensive carbon contribution at a high price per ton may not earn you a carbon neutrality claim, you'll be spared the risk of greenwashing accusations and litigation and will be part of a notable group of companies that have made similar commitments.

Frontier Climate began as a buying coalition between Stripe, McKinsey, Alphabet (Google's parent company), Shopify, and Meta (Facebook's parent company). These five companies committed $1 billion over ten years to fund the development and scaling of carbon removal projects at a guaranteed price of $1,000/ton. In 2022, they started to open up these projects to smaller companies and were joined by Canva, Skims, Boom Supersonic, Autodesk, and others. While it can be difficult to find, validate, and break into these projects on your own, groups like Frontier Climate are making it easier. You can either join efforts like Frontier Climate or ask your sustainability partner what options are available to participate in high-quality carbon removal projects.

In summary, if you are carbon neutral today and want to move an equivalent amount of money away from low-cost offsets and into more expensive carbon-removal projects, you will lose your carbon neutrality status. You will need to rethink how to communicate this change in your strategy to your executive team (who are not experts in sustainability but want what is best for the business) and to your customers (who may be used to a carbon-neutral badge on your products).

When having this conversation with your executives, be clear about the business goals you are focused on. To an executive with a basic knowledge of sustainability, the first argument that is likely to hit is that even if you lose carbon-neutral certification, you will gain brand legitimacy in this space by being associated with the highest-caliber sustainability projects on the planet. Share examples of companies around the world, and preferably in your industry, that have been fined for using cheap offsets to make undeserved sustainability claims. If you can convince your CFO that no additional expense is required (you're just moving budget from low-cost offsets to high-cost offsets); convince your Chief Legal Officer that you'll be further de-risking the company from any litigation or accusations of greenwashing (you're not making any carbon neutrality claim that a regulator or journalist can question); and convince your CEO that doing this will elevate your brand, they'll likely trust you to do the right thing.

Once you have internal buy-in, you'll need to turn to your customers to explain the change. Fortunately, you'll have the example of large companies to follow. In 2019, United Kingdom-based EasyJet made an impressive commitment to spend £25 million (about $32 million) each year on carbon offsets. This was a highly lauded decision, as the BBC even named EasyJet the "best airline for carbon emissions" in a March 2019 article. However, EasyJet soon came under fire from *The Guardian* and other newspapers that investigated the specific offset projects that EasyJet was buying and determined that a majority of them were "phantom offsets" or projects that had no additional impact on the environment.

EasyJet again made a bold decision as it adjusted its climate policy in light of new information. In September 2022, it announced that it would stop purchasing carbon offsets later that year. Instead, it would move, at minimum, that same amount of money into cutting edge carbon removal projects and industry-relevant low-emissions technologies like hydrogen-powered planes. This move showed true leadership from the team at EasyJet. They didn't falter in their climate commitments, even as they came under fire for making a mistake. Instead, they learned from the new facts presented to them and used them to reposition their strategy.

If your company already has a carbon-neutral commitment, consider repositioning yourself in the light of new facts.

> I'm practicing what I preach on this. I could have made this book carbon neutral and bought offsets at $20 per ton. Assuming each book has a carbon footprint of 5kg, it would have cost me about $0.10 per book sold to claim carbon neutrality. I wouldn't likely face any greenwashing accusations, though it's impossible to know how the future will judge us.
>
> But I'm going to do something different. Instead of moving $0.10 per book towards cheap offsets and claiming carbon neutrality, I'm going to move $0.10 per book sold towards biochar, a high-quality, expensive carbon removal project.
>
> I'll be paying over $120/ton for biochar, so I'm buying miniscule volumes per book (about .8kg per book sold.) While the book might not be carbon neutral, I feel good about the quality of the project I'm supporting. Read more at attainablesustainabilitybook.com/offsets

## DOS AND DON'TS IN COMMUNICATING ABOUT CARBON OFFSETS

If you decide to use carbon offsets early in your sustainability journey, you'll need to manage communication. Your executives (and especially your marketers) are going to be very excited to start talking about what they've done. They'll want to present it to the board, tell customers, and build a corporate social responsibility website to promote your carbon-neutral business.

Because this brings your role and your work into the spotlight and ties the company's brand and success to your success, this is to your advantage. But, if you don't manage it well, it can create a downward spiral of greenwashing. Once your company starts thinking of itself as a carbon-neutral business and talking about carbon offsets on every investor call, people will start asking questions. Were those offsets of a high quality? How many categories of Scope 3 were measured before the offset purchase? Below are some dos and don'ts to help you keep on top of communication at every stage of your sustainability journey.

DO:

- Talk about carbon offsets as a part of your sustainability strategy, not the entire strategy.
- Be transparent about the projects you supported and why those tie to your brand and goals.
- Be clear about which parts of your corporate emissions you are offsetting, if it's not the whole thing.
- Have your certificates of purchase available for customers to access.
- Talk about the company that helped you purchase these projects to make sure they are held accountable for any issues or quality concerns.
- Mention carbon offsets in relevant contexts to your customers, such as order confirmation emails.

DON'T:
- Act like carbon offsets save the world or absolve your company of any responsibility to reduce emissions.
- Make public commitments to being carbon neutral forever. As best practices and regulation around carbon neutrality claims evolve, you may not want to be carbon neutral in the future.
- Talk about offsets everywhere, all the time to your customers. The topic gets old if it's not approached tactfully.

As we've seen, carbon offsets are an important part of a modern sustainability strategy. They have gaps and flaws, but they are an integral part of corporate sustainability done well. Your company will need a point of view about using carbon offsets, making carbon neutrality claims, and communicating your strategy to stakeholders.

Carbon offsets, like the rest of your sustainability strategy, require leadership buy-in and support. In the next chapter, we'll look at the most common C-suite champions for sustainability and how to build the right business case for the right executive.

**SUMMARY**

- Your company needs a point of view on carbon offsets and carbon neutrality.
- There are dozens of types of carbon offsets that vary greatly in price.
- Carbon offsets can be seen as a self-imposed carbon tax against corporate emissions.
- Companies are starting to consider carbon contribution claims instead of carbon neutrality claims.

**ACTIONS**

Decide if carbon offsets fit your company's sustainability strategy. If they do, work with a partner to acquire offsets that feel meaningful to your company and check boxes around leakage, additionality, and permanence. Do not act as if being carbon neutral is the final goal of your sustainability strategy. At best, it is a self-imposed tax that you can be proud of and a step in your efforts to reduce and mitigate your emissions. At worst, it's just a tax and the cost of doing business.

*Chapter 7*

# BUILDING INTERNAL AND LEADERSHIP ENGAGEMENT

No corporate initiative goes very far without the leadership team being bought in. Sustainability is no different, even if it comes from a strong grassroots effort from a dozen employees. Even if it's a good business decision and a great marketing effort and seems like a good idea every way you look at it. As the head of ESG at a $10 billion tech company bluntly told me, "I'm not sure it's possible to have a successful sustainability program without executive buy-in."

In this chapter, we'll look at the different roles in the C-Suite and explore ways of getting each of them on board. We'll also look at the challenge of sustaining momentum and keeping up enthusiasm for sustainability efforts in the long run, as well as how to use these strategies if you're in a C-Suite position yourself.

The first step is to find your internal champion in the C-Suite. You know your corporate politics, and the unique personalities and interests of your executive team, better than most. So think strategically about who you want to approach with the idea of building a sustainability program. Depending on your choice, you'll want a different set of strategies and data to back up your goal of building a corporate sustainability program.

Often, the main executive champions are going to be the Chief Marketing Officer (CMO), the Chief HR Officer (CHRO) or Diversity, Equity and Inclusion (DEI) leader, the Chief Financial Officer (CFO) or Investor Relations (IR) leader), or the Chief Executive Officer (CEO). All other executives – operations, product leaders, sales executives – are less likely to see ROI from sustainability as directly as those four leaders. Each is focused on getting different results for the business so you need to know what they care about and present the set of facts that will convince them of the importance of sustainability for your company.

## CMO

The CMO is mostly focused on the company's brand and its relationship with stakeholders – often customers and prospects but also employees, partners, suppliers, and investors. Every decision the CMO makes is filtered through the question, "Will this improve or hurt what stakeholders think of my company?" If stakeholders see your company in higher regard, they are more likely to buy your products, work for your company, invest in the business, and reduce churn. Better brand, more successful CMO.

So when you approach your CMO, pitch sustainability initiatives in terms of improved brand. Depending on your industry, you may want to lean into trending consumer patterns, a competitive analysis, or any of a million studies that talk about sustainable businesses as more successful companies.

One of the best ways to get your CMO on board is to research what your top competitors are doing in sustainability. If there is one thing every CMO hates, it's to be outdone by the competition. So do the work for them and come to your pitch prepared with slides about what your top five competitors are doing for sustainability and how you stack up.

When you pitch your CMO:

1. Bring articles about why sustainability matters to your customers. If your customers demand sustainability, it makes the ROI clearer.
2. Do a competitive analysis to see what your top competitors are doing for sustainability. They won't want to fall behind the competition.
3. Look up the last five conferences your executives attended and see if they had a sustainability track. This proves that it matters to the industry and stakeholders at large.

## Case Study: Condado Tacos

*"Sustainability was important to Condado Tacos' employees from the beginning, so the company had always done its best to make sustainable choices. During consumer research, our loyalists credited us for our eco-friendly packaging and products and noted it as a factor in their loyalty – it made them feel better about their frequent to-go purchases.*

*As a marketer, I wanted to celebrate this aspect of our brand, learn how we could have an even greater impact and, honestly, get more credit for it. However, as I dug into our sustainability strategies and practices, I became less confident of whether there was a compelling story to tell and how to tell that story accurately for our brand.*

*We were a small but fast-growing company and no one on our side had this subject matter expertise nor the time to own this accountability, yet we understood the value for our company and brand and we desired to do better. We just needed a roadmap.*

*I wanted to continue to tell our sustainability story, but knew I needed stronger science and progress to stand on. So the ROI on finding a partner to help us accurately measure and start to reduce our emissions was pretty clear. I led the effort, had my CEO's support, and started investing in the hard work of sustainability so we could continue to deliver on our promises to customers and employees."*

- Sara Kear, CMO at Condado Tacos

## CHRO/HEAD OF DEI

The people leaders of an organization are focused on attracting and retaining top talent. That's all they care about, and that's all they want to hear about. They have one of the hardest jobs in the business, but also one of the clearest set of goals. They need to somehow convince great people to work for and stay at the company in one of the most competitive hiring environments in history. Success is straightforward. Hire people, good. Retain them, good. Lose them, bad.

In a competitive environment where money is limited (I'm sure the CHRO would love to increase salaries for everyone by 50 percent!), there are few ways within your control to win people over. CHROs can't change the kind of work the company does. They have little control over who your manager is. Benefits and perks are limited by capital.

That leaves just a few low-cost levers in the CHRO's arsenal: culture-building and employer-branding. If they can make the company seem like a great place to work and a place that values the same sorts of things that target employees care about, then maybe, just maybe, an employee will choose to work and stay at your company.

That's where sustainability comes in. Not every company can contribute directly to the fight against climate change. But if your CHRO can convince prospective employees that your company cares about the work and provides an opportunity to get involved, people who care about climate may choose your company over a competitor.

It's also why, in the absence of another leader, someone with a DEI (Diversity, Equity, and Inclusion) title is often the first to see sustainability as a strategic imperative. Just as DEI work went from a market advantage in the 2010s (of course diverse teams perform better!) to a market requirement in the 2020s (CEOs need to discuss diversity in investor conversations), sustainability is making the same leap from nice-to-have to must-have.

When you pitch your CHRO/Head of DEI:

1. Bring articles with data about employees wanting to work for a company seen as sustainable. Google "Fast Company millennials pay cut sustainability." That's a winner.
2. Poll a group of employees and ask them how much sustainability matters to them. Bring that data to your meeting. You can get even more specific data by organizing a sustainability event, like a park clean-up, and telling your people leader how much employees care about sustainability.
3. A competitive assessment helps here too. If your people leader learns about the sustainability programs at other companies in your industry, companies against which you are competing for talent, then they will have a business case to push for a sustainability program.

## Case Study: Culture Amp

*"If a company says that they are committed to equity and inclusion, that means in every area of their operations. Companies that are thinking about all stakeholders – as is increasingly expected by employees and customers – need to consider the fact that without conscious effort, their operations are likely impacting the environment and the future of our civilization in an inequitable way. The fact is, the status quo in our society is one of inequity. Companies that want to survive into the 2030s and beyond need to be investing in climate and environment in a real, tangible way to continue not only to be competitive but to exist at all given the escalating crisis we all find ourselves in."*

- Aubrey Blanche, Senior Director of People Operations & Strategic Programs at Culture Amp

## CFO / HEAD OF INVESTOR RELATIONS

Everyone thinks that the CFO is the hardest person to pitch on new initiatives. "CFOs are there to keep costs low and be strict on budget. CFOs are no fun! They never say yes to anything!"

That stops many people from pitching their CFO on a new initiative, even though the CFO has one of the easiest paths to finding and approving new budget. If you can figure out how to pitch your CFO in the way that matters most to them, you've got a strong chance at finding a truly powerful champion with direct access to the company's budget.

Your CFO has two jobs. Keep costs low and increase capital into the business. Sustainability, if run well, can solve both. Sustainability is all about reducing waste, which by its very nature means saving capital. No matter your industry, you can find examples of how a focus on sustainability has saved companies money.

As we saw at the start of this book, sustainability is also directly tied to successful fundraising. If your company has a sustainability program and is able to reduce climate risk, it meets the requirements for funding from large institutional investors, all of which need to know the carbon footprint of their portfolio companies. It shows your company is more ready for IPO (and any regulations that may be required of public companies) and is capable of raising money at improved valuations compared to your less-sustainable peers.

In publicly traded companies, it is becoming common to find a champion for sustainability in the Investor Relations leader. This person is on the frontlines of investor expectations. They're tracking what competitors are doing regarding ESG, aware of global investor expectations, and focused on keeping the company compliant with regulation. The Head of IR will often report to the CFO but still have their own budget to work with and a real business case for implementing sustainability. This makes them a great executive champion for sustainability work

When you pitch your CFO / Head of IR :
1. Find examples of waste around your company and show how sustainability can reduce them. Companies with large real-estate footprints can reduce their energy waste. Software companies can reduce their cloud storage costs. CPG companies can reduce packaging costs.
2. Bring together a list of institutional investors that focus on your industry and have sustainability requirements. Start by searching for "largest investors in [my industry]." Then go through the websites of the top ten investors and see how many have sustainability requirements. My guess is that almost any industry has more than 50 percent of investors with sustainability commitments to their limited partners (LPs). If your CFO believes the company can raise money faster if it has a sustainability program, they'll quickly find the budget.

## Case Study: bartaco

*"As CFO, I am always keeping an eye on regulatory and legislative actions and trends while focusing on initiatives that make us more profitable. Sustainability falls right between those two. It is very possible that companies like ours will soon be asked for sustainability data from regulators and investors (not to mention customers), so I need to make sure we remain nimble and prepared. And by reducing costly, wasteful emissions and attracting positive attention from customers and employees, a focus on sustainability can actually enhance our profitability and company culture, recruitment efforts and the guest experience.*

*bartaco has extra incentive to get this right. As we aspire to become a B-corp, we must make a binding commitment as a company to consider the environment right alongside financial profit. Maintaining our commitment to sustainability is a key initiative for our company and is the right thing to do."*

- Levi Martin, CFO at bartaco

## CEO

A CEO can be the most difficult person to get on board with a new initiative, but the one with the most influence to push it through. CEOs come in all shapes and sizes. Unlike their peers in the C-Suite, their focus isn't narrow. Depending on the stage of the company, the most recent challenge, and their own background and interest, they can be focused on anything from marketing to fundraising to product to cost cutting or literally anything else that anyone in the company does full time.

However, above all else, CEOs care about the long-term sustainability (in the non-climate sense of the word) of the company. Go to your CEO to pitch sustainability as something that will make your company more durable. Show them a mix of what you'd show to the other C-Suite executives.

The one thing that differentiates the CEO from everyone else is that they have a different boss. While everyone in the company eventually rolls up to the CEO, the CEO's boss is the board of directors. The board decides if the CEO stays or goes, decides if the CEO's compensation should be raised or lowered, and decides to approve or deny major budget commitments. So the CEO is always thinking about what the board might ask or expect of them.

You don't get many chances at pitching the CEO, so you don't want to waste their time. Think hard about what you know about your CEO and what matters most to them at this moment in time. Learn what they're most focused on and angle your sustainability pitch to solve that.

Research their personal connection to the environment. If they love spending time outdoors, have a close connection with nature, and show an affection for the planet, they are more likely to prioritize sustainability inside the company.

Additionally, research the board. If your company's board of directors has members who are on the boards of other companies with strong public sustainability strategies, they'll be champions of your company's sustainability focus. If your company's board has members who are known environmental donors, or represent investment firms with sustainability commitments or are CEOs of other companies with sustainability strategies, they'll be your allies in this pitch.

There is no clear template for pitching a CEO because they all have different backgrounds and different priorities at different stages of the business. If you can tailor your approach based on what you know about them personally and professionally and focus on the points that solve your CEO's most urgent problems, you'll have a good chance of winning them over.

## KEEPING LEADERSHIP ENTHUSIASM

Once you've won over your first executive sponsor of the sustainability program, it's your responsibility to keep them proud of your work and get other executives excited about sustainability. To keep your efforts funded and alive, you're going to want your executive sponsor to talk often about how successful your program is, and you will want other leaders from across the organization to come to you asking for help and ideas.

The first rule is consistency. You can't lose momentum on this project. Set up a monthly meeting of your green team where you'll all share updates on what you're focused on and challenged by. Invite your executive sponsor to join you at this meeting once per quarter. This sort of consistency is going to put momentum behind your program.

Next, focus on setting up at least one form of open communication. The simplest idea is a #sustainability channel in your company Slack or Microsoft Teams. If you and your green team are able to build a popular channel sharing sustainability tips, news, and ideas, it will prove how strongly the program resonates with employees.

Once you have a consistent setup and a forum for communication, focus on getting some quick wins on the board. Your executives are going to be inspired by action, not just ideas. While they may have given you approval to get started, via funding or just their blessing, you'll need to show them that this program is worth investing in. Steal ideas from Chapters 4 and 5 and do the easy things that show real ROI. Get a sustainability page up and running. Reduce energy emissions and utility bills through new habits among employees. Get rid of single-use plastics in the offices. Do something that is visible and tangible and exciting. Make sure that your executives know about this success. Use it to gain momentum and inertia for the next phase of your sustainability plan.

The last step in building internal engagement is to use sustainability to solve problems for other executives. Think of it as knocking down pins. You already won over one executive. Focus on making them proud of their decision. If you won the CMO as your sponsor, find some good marketing wins. Then work with the sales team to find the top ten prospects they're working on and research which have sustainability policies. Thrill your head of sales with the power of sustainability to move deals forward. Then move on to your operations team and find ways to improve something in that department.

Korn Ferry, one of the world's largest executive recruiting firms, published a thirty-page manifesto about the skills a great Chief Sustainability Officer should have. It said:

*"To take calculated risks – seizing any opportunity, large or small – a combination of passion, risk, intolerance, and resilience is essential. Be the spider in the web – know how to get traction at the highest levels. Shape, but don't deliver."*

CSOs are perceived as the "Chief Translation Officer," simplifying complex ideas and communicating the correlation between risk, trust, growth, and cost. Getting buy-in means articulating value for the business – an ability to "meet the business where it is at." They may not be the ones making the decisions but CSOs can achieve those goals through others with an ability to engage and inspire, and a willingness to fail fast and often."

This description fits your responsibilities, at any level of the sustainability org chart. Your job is to inspire other teams to take action. Take every win you can, and push for change. Different businesses find themselves at different stages of readiness, and you need to be creative and adaptable enough, and able to see decisions with enough business acumen, to push for the right change at the right time. You can't impose massive changes in the very first year of a sustainability program but you can inspire small changes across the business, use them to build a more comprehensive climate program, and show different teams the many opportunities in corporate sustainability.

### If you ARE the executive reading this:

You have the influence and budget to get your company's sustainability program started. You know where there's waste, you can identify targets for a sustainability effort, and you can ask your board what other companies do. Most importantly, you have the authority to make this a priority for a significant number of people.

First, you'll need sustainability champions to move things forward. Help them set up formal processes, like a green team, a monthly meeting, and a #sustainability Slack channel. Participate in the first few events – people will be more open to extracurricular activities if they see you doing it.

Sustainability should be the wind in your sails, not a breeze blowing you off course, so push for a win on a metric that matters to you. Don't start by creating KPIs, OKRs, or other sustainability-specific metrics. Make sustainability a tool that furthers your team's existing goals.

If you're the executive in charge of procurement and supply chain, you might want to reduce shipping times. So challenge your team to brainstorm everything from sourcing local suppliers and supporting higher-quality makers to reducing plastic and pushing suppliers to report on their sustainability metrics. Then select the project that reduces shipping times the most.

If you are the CMO focused on customer engagement, look at sustainability angles for outcomes you are already working towards. Have your teams pitch dozens of ideas, from a carbon-neutral product line or sponsorship of a sustainability-themed conference to becoming a channel for customers' environmental action. Then invest in the one most likely to increase customer engagement.

If your first sustainability effort becomes part of a successful campaign, as measured against your most important metrics, it will inspire others in your department. They'll be incentivized to find ways that sustainability can help support other key metrics, campaigns, and targets.

As the sustainability bug spreads throughout departments that report up to you, you'll want to create learning opportunities. Set up sustainability town halls where different teams can share their experiments and experiences, and bring department leaders together to collaborate on sustainability initiatives.

Tell your peers on the leadership team. At first, describe your work as a low-stakes experiment to see how your stakeholders react to sustainability, an experiment that might take time to bear fruit. This will avoid putting pressure on your team to succeed at all costs.

Finally, when you achieve real success, encourage other executives on your team to participate. Driven purely on its own merit, sustainability will become pervasive in every department and a natural lens for future decisions.

Sustainability programs simply will not succeed without executive sponsorship. Different functions have different reasons to care about sustainability, but you are most likely to find a champion in your CMO, CHRO, CFO, or CEO.

We've seen how helping them address the issue on their own terms is the way forward. Helping your executive use sustainability to find a win in the issue that matters most is the best way to build a business case for a more sophisticated program.

Once you've persuaded one or two execs, it should create a ripple effect throughout your company. And once you've got a thriving internal sustainability program, it's time to start looking at the most important level of all: policy.

## SUMMARY

- Sustainability programs will not succeed without executive sponsorship.
- You are most likely to find a champion in your CMO, CHRO, CFO, or CEO.
- Help your executive use sustainability to find a win on what matters most to them.

## ACTIONS

If you don't yet have executive buy-in, which of your company's leaders is most likely to support a climate program? Find ways to use sustainability to help them hit their current goals.

If you have an executive sponsor for your sustainability program, get their help in bubbling up the topic at executive team meetings and come up with ideas to get other executives on board.

If *you* are the executive, give your department the support and resources to bring sustainability into their work and reward them for using a sustainability framework in their core role.

*Chapter 8*

# POWER WIELDING

Nothing we've talked about in this book so far is going to help save the world. I know, I know. "What the heck, Adriel? I'm over one hundred pages in and you're telling me that everything I just read was a waste of time? I know there's only a handful of pages left, but why should I finish the book now that you've told me that?"

Well, it's not that nothing we discussed is important. It is. You need to have a strong grasp of your carbon footprint to succeed in today's market. You need to build your sustainability strategy with transparency at its core. You need to understand the differences between CDP and SBTi and decide which makes the most sense for your program. You need to be literate on carbon offsets and RECs and make thoughtful decisions to avoid greenwashing. All of this will help your business raise more money, hire better talent, and build stronger customer relationships.

And yes, it's definitely better for the planet if your business has a lower carbon footprint. Of course flying less or producing less waste or selling less meat makes an impact on climate change. It matters, and you're better off taking it seriously.

But here's the thing. Your little corner of the room, whatever room that is and however large a space you take up in it, is just part of a huge mansion. You control your corner, and you can influence the rest of your room, but it's hard to know what's happening in other corners of the house. And if we want our house, and all the people in it, to be stable and survive another 100,000 years, dusting our little corner is nice. Making sure our entire room is clean is important. But if a fire starts in any part of the house, we're all in trouble. The only solution is to fireproof the entire house. That scale of a solution can only come from cohesive, ambitious, and ubiquitous policy change, and your company has a role to play in this.

In my little housekeeping metaphor, knowing your carbon footprint is like dusting your corner of the room. It's just good business hygiene. Helping your supply chain become more sustainable and acting as a voice for your industry is like keeping the room tidy. If you act like a model citizen, your stakeholders will want to follow in your footsteps. That can create real change.

But true sustainability is bigger than any company or any industry. Companies that are truly serious about sustainability, the companies that insist on being leaders on this sensitive, complicated, and urgent topic, must think bigger. They must approach their task as one of power wielding. That means using their weight, voice, and financial influence to change systems, policy, and politics.

If the world is going to get serious about curbing the worst effects of climate change, true leadership needs to come from governments and regulators. Only through policy and regulation, ideally with global participation, can we really see carbon emissions drop to required levels.

So while businesses should absolutely focus on their own emissions, they also need to encourage government to push through policy changes. When a company throws its weight around and pushes through change at the policy level, it's called power wielding.

The term was introduced to me by Auden Schendler, Senior Vice President of Sustainability at Aspen Skiing Company (ASC). Let's look at how his business perceives power wielding. As ASC explains on its sustainability website:

*"Climate change is the greatest threat facing the ski industry, not to mention humanity. Changing light bulbs won't fix this problem; government must act. Our number one priority is using our voice, influence, and audience as a lever to drive policy change and to create the social movement to enable that change."*

It shared this same message with even stronger words in its 2021 sustainability report. Describing its approach, Aspen Skiing Company says its priority is to *"wield our unique power, reach, media appeal, and influence to drive large-scale change. Corporate operational greening and ethical behavior is important but insufficient to achieve sustainability and social equity. Because climate, race, and other issues are systems problems, they require systemic solutions."*

Of its many policy initiatives, its flagship program supports Protect Our Winters (POW). POW is a nonprofit organization focused on inspiring climate action across local, state, and federal governments. It organizes funding and voter turnout campaigns to support climate legislation as large as the federal government's $391 billion Inflation Reduction Act and as local as Colorado's House Bill 1261, a roadmap for the state to cut carbon pollution by 90 percent by the year 2050 compared to 2005 levels.

Aspen Skiing Company supports Protect our Winters through sponsorship, education, and marketing. In fact, it's so committed to the organization that it put the POW logo on all uniforms as a conversation starter and educational tool.

Aspen Skiing Company takes its commitment to policy change seriously. It's done all it can to reduce its own carbon footprint, from

LED lights to vegetarian meals to electric vehicle charging stations. That's all been important, and those impacts reverberate. But it knows that the snowy season will continually come later and be less predictable each year unless the whole world makes changes pushed by policy.

Another great example comes from the team at ButcherBox, a meat-delivery service with more than $500 million in annual revenue. It ships grass-fed beef, wild-caught salmon, and other high-quality meats around the country. By its very nature, it seems like sustainability would be a contradiction to ButcherBox's business. How can a company that ships heavy packages of meat and dry ice around the country, a company that contributes to emissions from two of the highest polluting industries (animal agriculture and transportation) speak with integrity about sustainability?

ButcherBox realized something important. For it to sell meat of the highest quality, it needs the land and sea to be protected. If land is overfarmed and animals are stuffed with pesticides, they won't provide customers with the quality of grass-fed meat they expect. If populations of wild salmon start to disappear due to climate change, ButcherBox won't be able to provide its customers with one of its most popular products. Climate change is very bad for ButcherBox's business.

But if the company can help shape the narrative around meat, and if it can influence policy to protect the slower, more sustainable processes needed to create the quality food it sells, it can make a meaningful difference on climate.

In that light, Evadne Cokeh, the VP of Social and Environmental Responsibility at ButcherBox, focuses on power wielding as a core part of the company's strategy. And it's had important wins to show for it.

ButcherBox sources wild-caught salmon from Bristol Bay, Alaska, one of the world's last safe havens for the fish. This is big business for ButcherBox as it makes tens of millions in revenue from it. If the ecosystem that supports the wild salmon disappeared, it would be a travesty for the ecology of the area and the economy of this company and its suppliers. So sustainability and environmentalism are very much in line with the company's profit motivations.

Environmental threats are far from hypothetical and in the mid-2000s, Bristol Bay was in danger. A mining company had discovered tens of billions of dollars of rare metals in the ground nearby and wanted to build a mine to extract it. The Pebble Mine would create a huge, short-term economic benefit, but at the cost of permanent ecological damage to the region.

The people of Bristol Bay had been fighting this mine for almost a decade. Some of the farmers and community partners that ButcherBox works with in the region reached out to the company to ask for help. They explained the situation with Pebble Mine and the risk to the community and the business. ButcherBox wanted to find a way to help.

In 2019, ButcherBox added its corporate voice to the many voices fighting the mine in Bristol Bay, including fisheries and citizens. It produced films highlighting the sacred environment of the region. It posted on social media with a highly-produced promotional video and references to on-the-ground organizations. It donated money to Trout Unlimited, the advocacy group behind the protection effort. It reached out to politicians and organized its community to do the same to stop the construction of the mine.

ButcherBox did not act alone here. They just put wind into people's sails, like their Bristol Bay fishing partners and organizations like Trout Unlimited, in whatever way they knew how. ButcherBox is a role model for corporate action and not just because it's a B Corp and a mission-driven company that impacted major environmental policy. It's a role model because it took a partnership approach, just like Aspen Skiing Company and Protect Our Winters, to help push for impactful policy change. It used its mission and its business to decide what to work for, and its resources to bolster others.

ButcherBox's sustainability leader, Evadne Cokeh, explained to me what a massive partnership effort this all was. "It was through our fishing partners that we first learned about Pebble Mine. It was through them that we learned about Trout Unlimited and were advised to support their work." When Evadne and I spoke, I tried to push her to take more credit for ButcherBox's role in the fight against Pebble Mine. From the outside, it seemed like they'd played a pivotal role. But Evadne thought that others deserved the credit. It was truer to the company's power-wielding strategy to put the spotlight on partners, she says:

"Yes, we have over $500 million in annual revenue. That's not insignificant, but we're not a huge company. We have 200 employees right now. We're not a behemoth. And the fight for Pebble Mine had been going on well before ButcherBox even existed. Our desire is to amplify the work that fishermen and nonprofits like Trout Unlimited have done. So the question we ask ourselves is, 'What is our role as a company? What does it mean to be a good partner?' Yes, this is part of our business. Yes, we sell salmon and would like to continue to protect that product offering. But at the end of the day, it comes down to listening to the needs of our partners, looking internally to see what we can do to support.

We have a charitable giving budget, we can sign petitions and put our voice behind it, and we can engage with our consumer base with interesting media to tell the story of this incredible ecosystem, giving them a call to action to get involved. Were we the ones that stopped Pebble Mine from happening? I don't know about that. There's a list of one hundred companies that fought against Pebble Mine. We were just one voice and one contributor."

In other words, the magic was not some mystical resource that ButcherBox has that other companies do not. It wielded corporate power driven by a strong partnership approach to push for systemic change.

After years of work from ButcherBox, and even more work from many smaller companies and private citizens, the EPA officially blocked the construction of the Pebble Mine. This was a massive win for the people, animals, and land of Bristol Bay. A true win for sustainability in the most straightforward meaning of the word.

But it was also a huge win for ButcherBox as a company. Set aside the marketing benefits of telling its customers (wealthy, educated Americans who care about the planet) that the company fights for the environment. Set aside the pride that employees must feel at a win like this, contributing to strong employee retention. Focus only on the numbers and the stakes were crystal clear. If the Pebble Mine had been constructed, ButcherBox would have lost tens of millions of dollars in revenue each year. This win for sustainability was, in pure economic terms, a win for the company.

ButcherBox doesn't think of its sustainability work in terms of profit and loss. Evadne doesn't have to run a spreadsheet model to justify support of Bristol Bay. It's just ingrained in its culture and way of doing business. Your company may not have a similar ethos. But if you need to show the financial benefit of any decision, you can almost always find ways in which climate change will affect your business and build your ROI case around that potential future loss.

I can almost see the gears turning in your mind.

You care deeply about sustainability and believe it would be inspiring for your company to take these sorts of actions. But you know it's not likely. Aspen Skiing Company and ButcherBox are relatively large companies that are basically in the business of environmentalism and sustainability. They can afford to throw their weight behind sustainability policy. It's good business for them.

But what if you own a small restaurant group or run social impact at an enterprise software company? Wouldn't it be near-impossible to take on similar efforts? You're probably right. For some companies, this kind of work would feel inauthentic. A cybersecurity company, for instance, should focus most of its policy work on improving internet regulation. If a marketing agency got involved in policy, why would climate be the place to start?

So let's dig into two ways to do this work that are within reach of any company: trade organizations and direct lobbying.

## TRADE ORGANIZATIONS

If your company doesn't have the resources or the willpower to move in a big way on climate policy, then one of the best things you can do is to join a relevant organization. Nearly every industry has multiple trade organizations focused on pushing relevant climate policy changes.

Joining these and donating your logo and a small amount of money to their effort legitimizes the trade groups' message to politicians. The more companies of relevance a politician hears from in her district, the more seriously she will take the demands.

A quick Google search for "[your industry] sustainability trade organization" will give you dozens of options to choose from. Take the Business Council on Climate Change, also known as BC3. A San Francisco-based climate collective, it brings together software companies like Google, banks like Wells Fargo, and utility provider PG&E to organize the local sustainability movement. It pools money from members to push for large-scale renewable energy deployments, runs educational events throughout the community, and works with local policymakers to push for sustainability-focused local regulation.

While BC3 is focused on a geographical community, almost every industry has an organization dedicated to helping that specific group with sustainability. The group Sustainable Travel International serves as a hub for knowledge and change across the tourism industry. With members like United Airlines, Internova travel agency, and boutique Portuguese hotel Pena Park, this group pushes sustainability throughout the travel sector. It hosts training, funds research, works with global policymakers, and coaches its members on sustainability best practices.

Joining these groups and playing an active role as a member and collaborator is a simple, low-cost way to wield your company's power and voice and push for change outside the four walls of your business.

## DIRECT LOBBYING

Perhaps the most important influence that your company can have on society's fight against climate change is on politics. Lobbying has been around for hundreds of years. Donating to campaigns that matter to a company, under the guise of doing the right thing for the American economy and the politician's constituents at large, is a well-trodden path.

Companies of different sizes and industries have varying amounts of influence at the policy level. As discussed in Chapter 1, the world's biggest investors are pushing the SEC to enact climate-reporting regulation. It shows what it means for a massively influential company to craft policy at the highest levels that will make an impact.

And as we've seen, ButcherBox, a mid-sized American brand with over $500 million in revenue, decided to put its policy efforts into local changes that affected its business and stakeholders.

But even small businesses can get involved on local levels to push change. In 2014, The Bullitt Center, an office building in

Seattle, Washington, lobbied for changes to the city's building codes to allow for more sustainable construction practices. The building, which was designed to be net zero in energy and water, helped to inspire new regulations that require all new buildings in the city to be built to similar standards. It pushed its city, Seattle, on changes relevant to its industry (construction) to make policy changes that would help the entire community.

In hundreds of communities across the country, grocery stores have pushed their local governments to ban the sale of plastic bags. In 2016 in Minneapolis, Minnesota, businesses got together under the leadership of The Wedge Co-op, a cooperative grocery in the area, to ask the city council to ban plastic bags from groceries across the city. The Wedge had banned plastic bags in its own store years earlier and wanted to use its success with the program and leverage in the community to push the rest of the city. While the proposal was passed that year, it took six more years of political lobbying, strong support, and soft pressure from the business community for the policy to take effect.

The business community played a few critical roles here. First, they were often the ones who pushed their local governments to consider the change at all. Local politicians listen to the strongest businesses in their area. And when a business with impact suggests a proposal, the local government will take it seriously.

Second, a local business can be a hub for educating and exciting the community on the topic. In the case of plastic bag bans around the country, the same grocery stores and retailers who first suggested the proposal were the ones who'd told their customers about it, encouraged local citizens to sign petitions and informed the community about upcoming city council meetings. Even in local government, where you might intuitively think that policy can move forward much faster than at the federal level, conflicting ideologies and competing priorities lead to lagging policy enactment. Businesses, which can take a longer-term view than individuals, can play a major role in continuing the forward momentum once the initial excitement has passed.

Lastly, local businesses can act as case studies and leaders. When politicians are uncertain if a law will be popular, or if it will help or hurt their constituents, businesses can use themselves as a testbed for experimentation. In Minneapolis's successful ban on plastic bags, it was the long-standing, self-instilled plastic bag ban at The Wedge Co-op that finally convinced other businesses and city council members that this policy change would not negatively impact the community.

Every company has a different level of comfort with being out in front, making policy on topics that are not directly and traditionally applicable to its business. It feels like the larger the company, the more is on the line if a stance goes wrong.

But there are multiple ways for companies to put the weight of their brands, dollars, and influence behind pushing for real change at the policy level. If you are uncertain about your company's appetite for taking a stance on a sustainability topic, start small. Join a local trade organization that wants to make an impact on something your employees and customers will universally and non-controversially appreciate, like a new bike path or a better composting and recycling program. Use that inertia to get your company involved in larger organizations pushing for more meaningful regulation and policy improvements.

Then, once you are ready to become a leader in the corporate fight against climate change, start to work with local, state, and federal policymakers on climate issues that are relevant and important to your industry.

As we've seen in this book, climate change permeates every aspect of our society. Restaurants can work with local governments to fight food waste. Software companies can work with states to introduce more renewable energy. Consulting firms can help their district representatives think through climate policy changes. Marketing agencies can encourage oversight organizations to more closely regulate greenwashing. No matter your company's industry or size, spend time thinking about meaningful conversations you can start with politicians at the relevant level to help fight climate change.

While reducing your carbon footprint is important, true change can only come from structural and societal movements driven by policy. Companies have a role to play through advocacy, education, and political action. You don't need to be out in front of a movement if that doesn't fit your brand. But supporting policy change – or power wielding – is the most important change you can make.

## SUMMARY

- Reducing your carbon footprint is important but true change is driven by policy.
- Companies have a role to play through advocacy, education, and political action.
- Supporting policy change – or power wielding – is the most important change you can make.

## ACTIONS

Find an organization that pushes for systemic change that your executives can get behind. It doesn't have to be a bold, controversial, political group. Get more bike lanes near your office. Vote in favor of funding to clean up a park. Support regulation for clean energy.

And your company can give more than just money. Vote. Write letters. Volunteer. Educate. There are many ways to support the political action and policy changes our society needs to see to combat climate change.

As you track the results of your power wielding, you'll see the world around you improving in measurable, meaningful ways.

# CONCLUSION

The great question of our time is, "Can we have it all?" Will capitalism prove adaptable enough to provide great wealth and prosperity to the world while also building a system that doesn't use more than the Earth can provide? Or will our great experiment collapse on itself and cause the world to start anew?

Can we have everything we want and maintain a healthy planet? Can we have the steakhouses, the flights around the world, the big homes, the golf courses, the cheap food, the cheap 24/7 electricity, and the two-car garages? Can I travel as often as I want, eat whatever tastes good, and buy new clothes when I want them while also calling myself an environmentalist? Can I avoid being a hypocrite while writing books printed in hardcover? Books that require people around the world to cut down trees, use energy to mill paper, and burn cheap fuel to ship them around the world to you, the reader.

I do not know the answer. Depending on the economist you listen to, capitalism is either, as Winston Churchill said, the worst system of its kind except for all the rest, or as an environmental purist might say, capable only of destroying.

From an optimist's perspective, I would hope that capitalism is adaptable. I would hope that we can come together in this decade and create meaningful, lasting, measurable change in how the world operates. I would hope that business leaders emerge and truly lead. I would hope that massive investments in a regenerative system will allow me to win my daughter's pride. I would hope for that.

But I do not want to use this chapter, nor this book, to convince you of the rosy picture that would serve my own interests. I will be dead in 50–70 years. The world is unlikely to implode in that time. That is more likely to be my daughter's or grandchild's problem. For the rest of my life, I can go on living, earning a great income, and eating meat on every flight without being affected. It's good to be an educated, wealthy American with the means to live wherever the natural disasters are not. I am fortunate.

So no, I do not think you should take me at my word when I say that capitalism, the system that created plastic-filled oceans and skyscraper-sized landfills, can also be the system that brings us to a sustainable Shangri-La. You can be skeptical when I tell you that human ingenuity is remarkable and I believe in a future of clean jet fuel, zero-emissions beef, circular-economy fashion, and low-cost direct air capture to offset everything that can't be reduced. I'm biased. I work in the industry. I want that to be true.

So instead, I'm going to make an argument in favor of unavoidability. Capitalism is flawed. And it is culpable. But it is also the source of too much good to go away. It has brought more people out of poverty, out of sickness, out of illiteracy than anything before. It has brought more choice, creativity, and convenience to the furthest reaches of the world than any system before it. Capitalism is the hand we've been dealt. And in the short time we have available to mediate the impact of climate change, our focus should not be on dismantling capitalism. It should be on improving it.

We need to focus on reducing our waste. Capitalism should love that, as less waste means more profit.

We need to focus on bringing supply chains closer to the consumer. Capitalism should love that, as it means lower transportation costs.

We need to rethink how our food system works, from farms to restaurants to groceries. Capitalism should love that, as it creates the opportunity for new products and marketing strategies.

We need to rethink when we maximize for the cheapest option

(clothing, consumer goods, carbon offsets) in favor of the highest quality. Capitalism should love that, as it creates both a reason to charge more in the short term and to innovate to bring costs down over time.

I believe it is possible. I believe we can have it all. I believe that having it all is the only path available to us. I might be wrong about all of this. But if I am right, we must act now.

# GET IN TOUCH

I wrote this book with one goal in mind: to inspire corporate leaders to start building their company's sustainability strategy. If you want to discuss what your company can do to get started, email me at: adriel@attainablesustainabilitybook.com
or visit: attainablesustainabilitybook.com for more information.

*Cheers to a greener future!*

## ACKNOWLEDGEMENTS

There are a lot of people to thank for this book, but it starts with my family. My parents, immigrants from the former USSR, taught me that I can have any level of change in the world that I want. I just need to put in the work and take the risk. And my wife, Abby, who told me early on that my best feature is my potential, and supports me as I do weird things like spend my early mornings and weekend days writing a business book. Thank you for your patience, I love you.

Speaking of family, thank you to my sister, Bashel Lubarsky (Instagram: @brushedbybash) for an amazing cover design. I love it. Thanks to Graham Southorn for your fantastic edits, to Jonas Peres for beautiful interior design (and a lot of revisions!) and to Emmalee Jones for making the book a very important 5% better at the last minute.

Many mentors have taken bets on me in the past that gave me the confidence to do something like this. Jeff Fisher, you were one of the earliest and most consistent. Wes Garrison, you repetitively lent support that I didn't know that I deserved. Alex Lassiter, thank you for bringing me into the climate world. It's a blast and an honor to work on something this important.

Many people taught me a lot about sustainability through interviews, as clients, and as reviewers of early drafts. Those include Mark Trexler, Greg Becker, Nick Stace, Mikayla Byfield, Rebecca Hoeflerr, Sophia Gluck, Robin Merritt, Simone Wren, Alex Harden, Auden Schendler, Evadne Cokeh, Sara Kear, David Robertson, Jeremy Globerson, Alyssa Walker, Aubrey Blanche, Ella McKinley, Rachael Claudio, Gary Chan, Ariel Cohen, Charlotte Flanagan,

Jeff Fromm, Jared Ingersoll, Ari Wienzweig, Michael O'Leary, Mia Kettlering, Sean McPhillips, Shane Dunne and so many others. Every conversation I have with leaders like you brings me hope and value. Thank you all.

Lastly, I want to acknowledge all the people working to push their companies to take action against climate change. Whether you act from a place of pure passion, good will, good corporate governance, or even reluctant rule-following, your work matters. Keep going and keep growing.

# BIBLIOGRAPHY

All charts and sources may be found at
attainablesustainabilitybook.com/charts

"Companies embrace employee sustainability education to tackle climate emergency," Fortune, https://fortune.com/2022/04/11/companies-embrace-employee-sustainability-education-to-tackle-climate-emergency/

"Management Teams Unprepared for SEC's Upcoming ESG Rule," IR Magazine, https://www.irmagazine.com/case-studies/management-teams-unprepared-secs-upcoming-esg-rule

"Our Fiduciary Approach to Sustainability and the Low-Carbon Transition," BlackRock, https://www.blackrock.com/corporate/sustainability/committed-to-sustainability

"Global ESG ETF Assets from 2006 to November 2022," Statista, https://www.statista.com/statistics/1297487/assets-of-esg-etfs-worldwide/

"Global Impact Report 2022," Zendesk, https://web-assets.zendesk.com/pdf/p-social-impact/Zendesk-Global-Impact-Report-2022-en-EN.pdf?_gl=1*icroat*_ga*ODI3NzA0NDU4LjE2ODk1MDgwMTI.*_ga_FBP7C61M6Z*MTY4OTUwODAxMi4xLjAuMTY4OTUwODAxMi42MC4wLjA.&_ga=2.248829058.423914496.1689508012-827704458.1689508012

"CO2 Removal Solutions: A Buyer's Perspective," McKinsey, https://www.mckinsey.com/capabilities/sustainability/our-insights/co2-removal-solutions-a-buyers-perspective

"Carbon Offsets: A License to Pollute or a Path to Net Zero Emissions?" *Financial Times*, https://www.ft.com/content/cfaa16bf-ce5d-4543-ac9c-9d9234e10e9d

"How BlackRock Made ESG the Hottest Ticket on Wall Street," *Bloomberg*, https://www.bloomberg.com/news/articles/2021-12-31/how-blackrock-s-invisible-hand-helped-make-esg-a-hot-ticket

"Best Buy's E-Cycle Program is Ambitious, Successful and Financially Unsustainable," *The Guardian*, https://www.theguardian.com/sustainable-business/2016/feb/23/best-buy-walmart-staples-ewaste-recycling-environment-landfill-electronics

"Corporate Responsibility & Sustainability Report 2023," *Best Buy*, https://corporate.bestbuy.com/wp-content/uploads/2023/07/FY23_CRS_Report.pdf

"The New Bottom Line: Money is No Longer a Dirty Word in Sustainability," *The Guardian*: https://www.theguardian.com/sustainable-business/2016/feb/23/corporate-social-responsibility-sustainability-general-mills-patagonia-ben-and-jerrys

"Examining the Business Case for Investing in Social and Environmental Change," *The Guardian*, https://www.theguardian.com/sustainable-business/series/the-new-bottom-line

"Rental Car Carbon Offset Program Proves Most Popular With Customers," *3BL CSRwire*, https://www.csrwire.com/press_releases/16088-rental-car-carbon-offset-program-proves-most-popular-with-customers

"The History of Carbon Offsetting: The Big Picture," *Impactful Ninja*, https://impactful.ninja/the-history-of-carbon-offsetting/

"Misleading ESG Claims – Will They Wash?" Cooley LLP, https://www.cooley.com/news/insight/2022/2022-09-27-misleading-esg-claims-will-they-wash

"Companies Accused of Greenwashing," *Truth in Advertising*, https://truthinadvertising.org/articles/six-companies-accused-greenwashing/

"How Private Equity Can Converge on ESG Data," BCG (Boston Consulting Group), https://www.bcg.com/publications/2021/private-equity-convergence-on-esg-data

"A Blueprint for Scaling Voluntary Carbon Markets to Meet The Climate Challenge," McKinsey, https://www.mckinsey.com/capabilities/sustainability/our-insights/a-blueprint-for-scaling-voluntary-carbon-markets-to-meet-the-climate-challenge

"Briefing: Legal Risks of Carbon Offsets," ClientEarth, https://www.clientearth.org/media/lcvhm5uw/carbon-offsets-legal-risk-briefing.pdf

"Climate Change: Which Airline is Best for Carbon Emissions?" *BBC News*, https://www.bbc.com/news/science-environment-47460958

"2020 Social & Environmental Assessment Report," Ben & Jerry's, benjerry.com/about-us/sear-reports/2020-sear-report

"Ryanair Accused of Greenwash over Carbon Emissions Claim," *The Guardian*, https://www.theguardian.com/business/2020/feb/05/ryanair-accused-of-greenwash-over-carbon-emissions-claim

"Chef Accuses Michelin of "Greenwashing" Over New Sustainability Icon," *Restaurant*, https://www.bighospitality.co.uk/Article/2020/03/05/Chef-accuses-Michelin-of-greenwashing-over-new-sustainability-icon

"KFC Unveils New Solar-Powered Drive-Thru," *The Takeout*, https://thetakeout.com/kfc-bakersfield-california-new-solar-powered-drive-thru-1850072169

"The Rise of the Chief Sustainability Officer," Korn Ferry, https://www.kornferry.com/insights/featured-topics/people-planet-profit/the-rise-of-the-chief-sustainability-officer

"Keurig Canada to Pay $3 Million Penalty to Settle Competition Bureau's Concerns Over Coffee Pod Recycling Claims," Government of Canada, https://www.canada.ca/en/competition-bureau/news/2022/01/keurig-canada-to-pay-3-million-penalty-to-settle-competition-bureaus-concerns-over-coffee-pod-recycling-claims.html

"Puma's Chief Sourcing Officer on Upgrading Brands' Sustainability Marketing," *The Business of Fashion*, https://www.businessoffashion.com/articles/sustainability/the-state-of-fashion-2023-report-puma-sustainability-marketing-sportswear/

"Responsible Investing: A force for good", Hg, https://hgcapital.com/responsibility/

"Plant-Based Foods Market to Hit $162 Billion in Next Decade, Projects Bloomberg Intelligence," *Bloomberg*, https://www.bloomberg.com/company/press/plant-based-foods-market-to-hit-162-billion-in-next-decade-projects-bloomberg-intelligence/

"Fake Meat Sales are Growing, but Is It Really Better for You?" *Fortune*, https://fortune.com/2015/05/11/meatless-meat-sales/

"Size and Impact of Resale 2021," ThredUp, bit.ly/thred

"The Green Premium," Breakthrough Energy, https://breakthroughenergy.org/our-approach/the-green-premium/

"Leonardo DiCaprio Addresses Climate Change at the Oscars," *EHS Today*, https://www.ehstoday.com/environment/article/21917384/leonardo-dicaprio-addresses-climate-change-at-the-oscars

"Manchester United, Arsenal, Leeds: Will footballers' green armbands make fans take climate action?" *Euronews*, https://www.euronews.com/green/2023/02/04/manchester-united-leicester-city-chelsea-football-teams-call-on-fans-to-help-them-win-gree

"How ESG Investing Came to a Reckoning," *Financial Times*, https://www.ft.com/content/5ec1dfcf-eea3-42af-aea2-19d739ef8a55

"One Small Step To Reduce Plastic, One Giant Leap Toward Zero-Waste," *Forbes*, https://www.forbes.com/sites/lauratenenbaum/2019/10/02/one-small-step-to-reduce-plastic-one-giant-leap-toward-zero-waste/?sh=5f1ab8d325b4

"Uber Eats Revenue and Usage Statistics (2023)," *Business of Apps*, https://www.businessofapps.com/data/uber-eats-statistics/

"In War on Plastic Waste, New York City Council Strikes a Blow," NRDC, https://www.nrdc.org/experts/eric-goldstein/war-plastic-waste-ny-city-council-strikes-blow

"Brad Smith Explains Why the World Needs to Go Carbon-Negative — and How to Get There," *Protocol*, https://www.protocol.com/climate/brad-smith-microsoft-president-sustainability

"Encouraging New Choices Through Incentives for Electric Vehicles," Apex: https://www.apexcleanenergy.com/insight/encouraging-new-choices-incentives-electric-vehicles/

"Publishers Are Seeing Increases in Advertiser Requests around Climate and Sustainability Coverage," *Digiday*, https://digiday.com/media/publishers-are-seeing-increases-in-advertiser-requests-around-climate-and-sustainability-coverage/

"10 Big Findings from the 2023 IPCC Report on Climate Change," World Resources Institute, https://www.wri.org/insights/2023-ipcc-ar6-synthesis-report-climate-change-findings

Milton Keynes UK
Ingram Content Group UK Ltd.
UKHW022204080324
439162UK00014B/756